THE ADVENTURES
OF A
SAN FRANCISCO
NEWSMAN

Baron M. Muller

Published by Don't Call It Frisco Press

Cover design by Richard Sigberman

Design and production by Waldo Freen

Set in 10 point Bookman. Reproduced from pages generated on the Macintosh II computer and printed on the Apple LaserWriter QMS-PS 810.

ISBN 0-917583-21-3

Printed in the United States of America

Dedication

To Patty A. Sterling of San Jose, a wonderful and loving daughter. She has always been one of my special boosters, from her college days when she first began reading my "stuff," she started urging that I put my experiences on paper. She never let up until I finished the last chapter of this book. And to my son, Barry Allen Muller, a loving task master who saw to it that I followed a rigid and daily writing schedule.

Also, special thanks and appreciation to my dear Niece, Dolores Cassady of Foster City, who kept reminding, "... Unkie....keep going on that book."

Forward

Murder and Mayhem

The gorgeous young wife and dancer, screaming and scratching for her life, was pinned nude on her bridal bed and was savagely being tortured with scalpel and searing acid by her insanely jealous doctor, bridegroom. The husband, recently arrived from Hungary, had not completed his medical requirements and was limited only to practice as an anesthesiologist. When the police broke down the door of the couple's apartment, they shuddered and froze at the sight of the mutilation being performed on the bride. The doctor stood by without any sign of emotion and boastfully declared, "She won't die...I'm a doctor...I know just how far to go. No man will ever want to look at her body again."

The year was 1963 and the crime is still listed in newspaper files as: "The Case of The Acid Bride." It was the most grotesque killing and trial I ever covered.

Eleven years later the horror was almost duplicated in an equally malignant murder and torture that happened in a home on Potrero Hill, overlooking San Francisco Hospital.

The killer, Angelo Pavageau, is still trying for the sixth time, to get out of prison on parole. The victim, a 25 year old food store assistant manager was bound to a dining room chair and bludgeoned to death with a heavy cutting board.

His wife, also 25, was dragged to her bedroom, raped, sodomized and beaten into unconsciousness over a period of three hours. Pavageau picked up several pieces of valuable family jewelry, set the house afire and left. The wife regained some of her senses minutes later and saved herself by climbing out of a bedroom window and dropping to a garage roof below. She still expects a return visit from the killer, according to police inspectors. These summaries are so terrible it is hard to believe they actually happened...they did...without any exaggeration.

Every day started with a blank piece of copy paper in the typewriter and we never knew what to expect and why, however it was not always days of fun and laughter. Horror could be, and sometimes was, too present. After a distressing story did appear in print, most of us were professional enough to put the "bloody days" out of mind, and thus keeping from becoming too cynical. The only stories I brought home were the funny and the naughty ones. When I was invited to a cocktail party my friends would gather round and ask for these stories. I sometimes thought, "...the best stories are the ones we couldn't print."

Three heinous murder cases, with all the horrors included, are presented in this book, not for shock or sales appeal, but to show how homicides have changed so little with the passing of time. I believe that only three factors seem to have changed...the date of the crime, the name of the victim and what instrument of death was used.

Each generation of news writers and readers hopefully learn something from the last. History is a good story and the truth is the best story to learn. That's one of the reasons I wrote this book.

Table Of Contents

1. Attempts To Enter The Fourth Estate   1
2. Sick On The Street   5
3. First Meeting With Sally Stanford   6
4. A Lecture On News Writing   12
5. G.B. Shaw Comes To Town   13
6. How News Gets Born   17
7. Central Emergency, A Most Important
    Beat   19
8. The Sidewalk Question Man   21
9. Walking The Golden Gate Bridge Catwalk   22
10. Meeting The President   26
11. San Jose Lynching   29
12. Captain Ahab   34
13. The Frank Egan Case   38
14. April Aaron: Senseless Violence Hits
    The Streets   44
15. Krushchev Comes To Town   46
16. Executions At San Quentin   48
17. Baron Meets "Baron"   56
18. The Frenchman Gets His Citizenship   59
19. Bianchi Gets HIs License   62
20. Case Of The Acid Bride   64
21. Angelo Pavageau Murder Case   70
22. Bridge Jumpers   74
23. The Best Fire Department   76
24. Long Weekend At The Nudist Camp   82
25. Watching A Rare Heart Operation   85
26. Our Own Esprit de Corps   88
27. Joe DiMaggio Marries Marilyn   90
28. President Johnson Gets Sworn In   94
29. Getting Out Of The Trenches   96

Preface

This book was written with the hope of entertaining my readers with tales from everybody's favorite city.

It was never written to serve as an autobiography, a local history or a journal of news stories that happened in San Francisco over the past forty-five years.

Also, it was never my intention to edify any readers, but instead, to possibly amuse anyone interested in this era.

The Adventures are written in vignette style on purpose, to hold reader interest...never to bore. The stories have been selected at random from my memory, in no special order and all are tales I personally covered. My career started on The News, merged into the News-Call Bulletin and finally combined with The Examiner, "The Monarch of the Dailies." I never left home.

Baron Muller, new staff member of the San Francisco News.

CHAPTER 1

Attempts to Enter
The Fourth Estate

On a pretty afternoon in late June I departed Palo Alto for San Francisco to learn if I had the attitude and training to become a newspaperman. The year was 1932. My Stanford sheepskin, that's what we called a bachelor of arts degree then, was tucked under my arm and I had no doubts about my writing ability.

I didn't picture myself as another Richard Harding Davis, the famed correspondent, but my spirits were high and I felt capable of turning out copy that would satisfy most editors.

During my rounds of the four papers, there were two morning and two afternoon papers then, the question most often put to me was, "How come you're so eager to get in this business?" I told them, "My family are bankers and I want to get away, as far as possible, from that stuffy world of sexless finance." It was a field I knew I would soon come to hate.

My dad was a Vice President at the Old Crocker Bank on Montgomery Street, later taken over by Wells Fargo. My Grandfather, on the maternal side, was one of the founders and directors of Franklin Savings and Loan Society, the oldest and most conservative institution of its kind here. With that background, my family naturally assumed that following college I would step into the field of finance. They had no doubts about my future. Worst of all, they never asked me.

During my senior year at Galileo High School, I started to realize that the world of finance was not for me, and was not going to be my life's work. I knew then I had to get away, as far as possible from dusty ledgers and countless numbers.

I had read "City Editor" by Stanley Walker, who is said to be the toughest and most exacting newsman in New York. I was fascinated. Next came the play, "Front Page." Now I felt hooked, and sat through it several times, along with the equally thrilling movie version.

Meanwhile, in my senior year in high school I unexpectedly won the annual short story contest. That was a great ego builder. Later, when I entered Stanford I was one, of only five, in the freshman class, to pass the English essay entrance exam. That cinched it for me. My mind was made up. I was going to be a newspaperman.

Stanford, at that time, had no bachelors degree in journalism as such, and to get around that, I took most of the courses available in English, newswriting and communications. Any spare time was spent on the staff of the campus paper, "The Daily." In due time I graduated and was sure of where I was going. I started my job hunting quest in San Francisco.

The Examiner, everyone agreed, was the outstanding and most quoted paper in the city, so I trooped over to Third and Market Street and presented myself to the Managing Editor, who was patient enough to give me an interview. He took me out into the city room, and said, "Son, see all those empty desks, we're right in the middle of a depression now and we had to let so many people go. I would love to give you a job, but we just haven't any openings at this time. Come back in a couple of years when the depression is over and maybe we can find something for you." The next place I visited was the San Francisco Chronicle at Fifth and Mission. There I got the same story and once again was shown the empty desks. I vowed I was not going to be discouraged.

The managing editor waved at the empty desks and said, "Son, I don't want to discourage you but, the staffer that has been laid off last will be the first one re-hired. You've got a lot of competition ahead."

The city had four large and financially healthy papers at that time, two mornings: The Examiner and Chronicle and two afternoons: the Call Bulletin and San Francisco News, a Scripps Howard paper. The next one I tried was the Call Bulletin, a Hearst paper and again got the cold reception, "...nothing doing here."

Finally I went over to The News at 4th and Mission streets. Then, there was no such thing as tight security with locked doors and armed guards. I walked right in and had a face to face talk with the Editor, W. N. "Bill" Burkhardt, one of the finest newspaper men I have ever had the pleasure of working with. He was a real gentleman.

He gave me the same bleak story about the depression. I listened politely and then startled him with, "Mr. Burkhardt, I'll work for you for nothing. I have to find out if I have the stuff for becoming a newspaperman." I added, "I'm in a fortunate financial position, I'm living at home in the Marina District with a family able to support, feed and clothe me, and I think I can do a good job for you, on a trial basis of course."

He leaned forward with a puzzled expression on his face and said: "...do you mean that...are you serious? No one has ever made that kind of offer before."

I assured him that I was never more serious and we shook hands on the deal. He led me by the arm through the news room and introduced me to City Editor Morton Sontheimer. "Sonty," he said, "you have a new staffer, put him to work."

Morton Sontheimer; we called him "Mort" or sometimes just "Sonty," was most able, seldom held a grudge and looked like a movie city editor of that time, later played so well by Clark Gable.

At that time there was no Newspaper Guild or Writers Union and every new reporter tried to negotiate the best deal possible for himself. Working for nothing was unheard of. Today, such a deal would be impossible.

Some of the staff resented me at first and felt, because I was working for free, I was taking a job from a laid off and needy veteran staffer. Another gripe was that I started as a reporter and never climbed the ranks up from the lowly job of copyboy.

Sontheimer was told to "put me to work" and that he did. It was more like "through the wringer." I got most of the dull and unwanted assignments, including listing the names of all newly elected officers and directors of the many improvement and fraternal organizations in the city at the time. Most of these stories, called "overnighters" and written for the next day, seldom saw print. There were too many. Enthusiasm was one of my major assets. I was eager to learn. When a fire alarm box came tapping in or an accident was reported, I was first to volunteer, "...let me go, I want to learn." I knew I had to get out and pick up some "street smarts." There was no better place to learn.

Every day during my trial period on the paper, I could feel the pressure of the job slowly mounting. It's an unpleasant feeling to arrive at work and know your job is on the line and today may be the last day of your career of dreams. I didn't have the guts to ask any of the associate editors or staffers, "...how am I doing? and none of them gave me the pleasure of a pat on the arm and the assurance of, "...Kid, you're doing a good job, keep it up."

CHAPTER 2

Sick On The Street

The first time I got sick on the job was at an accident story. It was a sticky summer afternoon and we were alerted to a "bad one" in front of the St. Francis Hotel. A well dressed man, trying to beat a cable car across the street, caught his heel in the cable slot and fell under the front wheels of the car. The ambulance and I arrived at the same time and we were surprised to see the man sitting up and staring at the mashed stump of left leg that had been severed at the knee. I walked over to the corner sewer and became ill. That was the last time. I often thought the trauma was so horrendous that it blocked all biological urges in the future.

Sontheimer was also a good teacher and had his own way of impressing details on you. You never forgot his method. To him it was a cardinal sin to spell a person's name wrong in print; and to make the big impression on any offender, he waited until dinner time, would interrupt your meal with a phone call and tell you about the mistake. Most of the staff never got a second call.

In addition to "street smarts," I soon learned the importance of contacts and news sources. The star reported never sat at the bar huddled over a drink waiting for a mysterious man to tap him on the shoulder and whisper, "I've got the big one for you." Likewise the reporter never grabbed the phone off the back bar and screamed to his city editor, "Hold the presses." That never happened.

It would have been wonderfully simple if we could sit at our desks, gaze into a crystal ball and conjure up what was going on about town. The best way was to have people talking to you. The more contacts, the more stories.

CHAPTER 3

First Meeting with Sally
Stanford

Sally Stanford was one of my most reliable and trusted sources of news in the years ahead and a good friend until the day of her death. I always regarded her as a delightful and feminine woman and most wise in the ways of the world.

I met her, of all places, at a fire. On that special morning, just before seven, a fire call ticked out on the alarm box in the office. The code book showed it to be Sally's apartment on Geary Street, adjoining Islam Temple Shrine headquarters. I had heard much talk around the office concerning her but hadn't met her yet.

Someone called out, "...it's a fire at Sally's whore house." I answered back, "...can I go?" The boss grinned and said, "...sure kid, why not? It's time you met the old gal."

I got there as the fire engines pulled up. Sally and three girls were already on the sidewalk, shivering in their scantiest and skimpy robes. All dollies three, the girls were living in the apartment and available for "anything" at all hours.

The fire was reported as a "nothing," a shorted toaster that gave off clouds of smoke. Sally and I started to talk while the firemen were picking up their gear and we hit it off rather well.

She always liked men, she confided, especially young men and added, "...would you like to come up for a little breakfast after the smoke is gone?" "Sure," I blurted.

Sally led me upstairs and I used her phone to tell my office the fire was a "no story." When I added I was invited to stay for breakfast, the reply was, "...good for you...take your time."

Sally prepared coffee, toast and sweet rolls while we talked. I still recall that morning as the

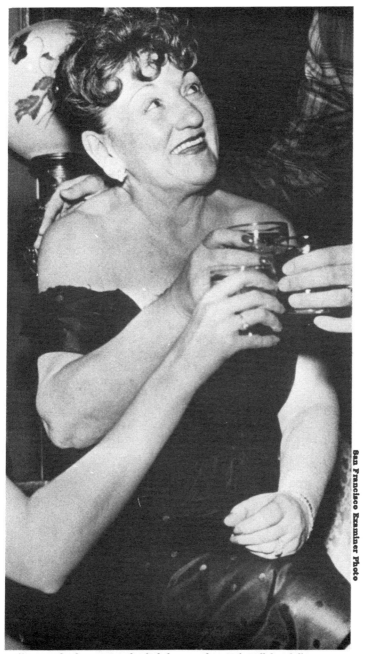

Sally Stanford toasting the holidays at her Nob Hill bordello.

beginning of a friendship that lasted a lifetime.

Since I was a Stanford man I was anxious to hear how she got the name of Stanford. "I'll tell you," she laughed. "One Sunday morning I was reading about the Stanford football team winning the Big Game. There's a classy name I thought, I'll take it. After that, I've always been Sally Stanford."

Sally was short, perhaps a bit overweight but nevertheless most attractive. She had the speech and manners of a Mae West, including the swagger.

The price of a visit to most brothels in town then was two dollars. Sally charged three. She believed her girls were "better" and "worth that much more." In the years ahead after Sally became more infamous the price of a trick rose to twenty-five dollars. A weekend jaunt with only one girl would start at a hundred bucks but more often ended up costing much more on account of the "extras." The girls said they preferred the week-long jaunts as "the tips were always more generous."

After the War, Sally decided to go first class. She moved her base of operations up to Nob Hill into a ritzy stone mansion fashioned after an old English fortress. The entrance was a massive iron gate, including a private phone line connected to Sally's phone bank. If she didn't know you, you didn't get in.

Sally liked company and once in a while, not too often, she would call and purr, "Baron, drop around and have a cup of tea." I didn't drink-that would have made it too hard to leave. A couple of times a year, usually in the afternoon when there was no hot news breaking, I'd drop by for a visit.

Sally was never secretive in telling about the way she operated. She ran a "call house" which meant, when a customer phoned for a particular honey, the girl would respond to the customer by cab, usually to a local hotel.

Sally worked out of her elaborate living room and had many phones within arms reach in front of her on a French provincial coffee table. Nearby was a stack of photo albums filled with jumbo size pictures of her girls, in color of course, wearing revealing

evening gowns or less. They were gorgeous.
The usual procedure, as I've already explained, was to phone in and make a date, that is if Sally knew you. Quite often a customer would show up in person and make a selection from the photos while reclining on a king sized divan with a drink. When the selection was made, Sally called her girl, usually at home and gave directions where to report for work.

The girls were so charming and ladylike too that they would never have been suspected of being, what they sometimes called themselves, "Ladies of the Evening."

Many of the girls had husbands holding down night jobs. The girls had no qualms about their "work", they knew they'd never be missed at home for a few hours and best of all the money was too good to pass up. Sally talked about her youth in the Midwest and her real name Mable Janis Busby, later Marsha Rapp. Several other marriages, with fitting name changes came along and didn't last too long. Best of all she liked being called Sally Stanford.

In 1951 she shocked the social set here when big headlines screamed of her elopement to Reno with Robert Livingston Gump. He was a member of the prominent family that owned and operated "Gumps", one of the leading art dealers in town. The name, Sally Stanford Gump delighted her but the marriage didn't last too long either.

She pulled another big shocker in 1961, when she quit the madam business, moved to Sausalito and opened one of the most successful restaurants in Marin, The Valhalla.

She got out of the "Business", she explained later, when her two adopted children were getting old enough to ask embarrassing questions about her. All along she had kept them away at exclusive boarding schools, and soon they would be coming home. It was time to leave the city behind. She knew she had to show them respectability.

She ran the restaurant like a queen and instead of sitting on a throne, she converted a heavily upholstered barber chair into a throne. The chair was placed so that she could survey not only the entire cafe, but the front door as well to greet her arriving guests. Often she sat with her pet parrot perched on her shoulder.

The wine list was outstanding and the food excellent, but I didn't eat there too often. I wanted to avoid taking advantage of her hospitality. Whenever an old friend dropped by, she insisted on picking up the tab.

When my daughter Patty turned twelve, I took the family over to dinner. Sally saw me walking in and stepped off her barber chair and gave me a big hug, including a kiss. After we were seated, my daughter turned to me and asked, "...Daddy, I didn't know you knew the lady that well...how come?" As best as I could I explained, "Honey, she's just another source

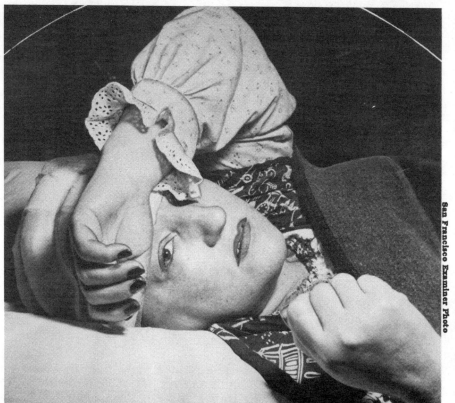

Sally Stanford in the '40s aftre being mugged and robbed of her jewels.

of news."

Sally proved to be a successful businesswoman, no matter what type of enterprise she entered. The Valhalla was hers and she took personal charge of all details.

Every morning she arose at dawn, drove to the wholesale markets and selected the best meats and produce. Every bit of food had to be "Grade A," she insisted. That was her way. "That's a carry over from my call house days," she would laugh.

Sally still felt she needed a bit more of respectability. The best way to get it was to run for public office. Her campaign for mayor turned bitter with many voters objecting to her background and reputation in San Francisco. She kept in the race and when the votes were counted, she even surprised herself by getting elected to the office of Vice Mayor of Sausalito. The new title was hilarious to her and she had business cards printed with the name "Vice Mayor" in raised bold type. She topped that later by getting elected Mayor.

Less than a year before she passed away, the members of the papers, radio and TV here decided it was time Sally was honored with a dinner at the Press Club. She was starting to show her age and the press felt a special tribute was long overdue to show "thanks" for all the stories she had given. The night was September 3, 1981. The party was a great success with some standing three deep in the rear of the hall. As speaker of the evening, I kept reminding Sally she was, "San Francisco's finest and best loved Public Utility." Tears filled her eyes. She died February 1, 1982.

CHAPTER 4

A Lecture On News Writing

Days after I first met Sally Stanford, I faced my first lecture on writing proper newspaper English.

Sontheimer handed me a press release on an upcoming phone rate to be held before the State Public Utilities Commission, and asked for a three hundred word story on the pending hearing.

I walked back to my desk, determined this was going to be my big opportunity to showcase my Stanford education. I wrote, rewrote and polished that piece till it seemed perfect, and then dropped it in the wire basket on the city desk. Out of the corner of my eye I watched him read my "beautiful" copy. Following the second reading he let go with a blast, "Baron, come here." Up I went and the lecture began. "Kid, remember, you're not writing for the Stanford Review, and you're not writing a thesis for your doctorate..You're writing to the level of our subscribers, most of whom only have an eighth grade education...so write accordingly." Simple English is always effective English, he explained.

One of the most poignant passages in the Bible reads, "...and Christ Wept." "Use the simple prose of Pearl Buck, especially her novel, "The Good Earth." That's one of the better examples of good writing."

As I walked back to my desk, I realized how little I knew about newswriting. The stuff I had learned in college was just a mere beginning. I became a firm believer in on-the-job-training.

CHAPTER 5

G. B. Shaw Comes To Town

I was still in limbo on the cashier's payroll records when the great George Shaw arrived on the liner, "Empress of Britain." He was to spend a fortnight at San Simeon as the house guest of publisher William Randolph Hearst. Before he disembarked, Mr. Shaw held a lengthy press conference in the lounge and gave the reporters a chance to quiz him in depth. Our top reporter handled the interview for The News and did an outstanding story, I thought.

Sontheimer wasn't too pleased with the piece. "Baron," he said, "I've never been a Shaw fan, and I'd like to take a little of the stuffiness out of his makeup. Go down to the ship and ask a simple question...the sillier the better...something to show he might be human after all." I was still bucking to get on the payroll and knew it would be fatal to refuse the interview. I had no idea of the question I was going to ask so I answered with a "Sure."

At the stateroom section of the luxury suites the purser blocked my way with the explanation, "Mr. Shaw is packing to depart for San Simeon. The press was here two hours ago, the interviews are over."

"I don't want to interview him," I explained. I just want to ask him a couple of questions."

The purser threw up his arms in disgust and again loudly announced, "Mr. Shaw won't see you." He abruptly turned and left that section of the ship.

I couldn't go back to the office without an interview, ...it was must...I knew. No purser was going to shut me out. The best way to locate Shaw, I reasoned, was to walk down the passage way and knock on every stateroom door I passed.

At the eighth door I tried I heard a crisp voice announce, "Come." I pushed open the door and was surprised to find I was looking into the beard of Mr. Shaw. He looked like a shaggy billy goat and then the question I was seeking come to mind. It was hard to keep from laughing in his face.

When I introduced myself he cut me short with, "I'm leaving the ship now and you'll have to leave too, the interviews are over."

"I don't want to interview you, Mr. Shaw," I interrupted, "but I would like to ask you one question."

"What's that?" he asked.

"My readers would like to know if you sleep with your beard under the blankets or on top of the bed covers at night?"

His face turned livid and I expected he was going to strike at me, or have a seizure.

"Young man," he hissed, "I'm deeply insulted. Leave now or I'll call the porter," he threatened and pushed me out of the stateroom. All through school I had read and heard about Mr. Shaw's delightful sense of humor and I expected a laugh or a comical retort, but never the anger in his voice and face.

I left in despair feeling I had blown my opportunity at a big story and my chances of getting on the staff was now zilch. The office would expect me to turn in some kind of a story and so I wrote: "One question of world burning importance went by the boards today as George Bernard Shaw departed for San Simeon as the guest of William Randolph Hearst;" I wrote on filling in the details and ended with the big one about his beard. I turned in the story and waited for the blast. As usual, it was "Baron", and I approached with the sickly feeling of thinking here's where I catch it.

Sontheimer asked, "You really put that question to him?" With a sickly grin on my face I answered, "Yes." He jumped up, grabbed my hand and smiled, "Just what I wanted, it's great and should go in a page one box." Then he took my arm and walked me into the office of Editor Burkhardt, told him about the Shaw story and added, "Baron did one hell of a job on this story. I like his attitude of not giving up and I recommend we keep him on the staff." Burkhardt agreed and said, "Now that you're on the staff, drop by the cashier's cage on your way home and pick up the checks for the weeks you've been sweating here."

George Bernard Shaw

I felt great and so did the staff. I was accepted and to show my thanks I invited everyone down to Schmalt's Bar on the corner and set up drinks for everyone. Sontheimer was the first in line.

The story drew a big laugh in press circles and a couple of reporters had the nerve to claim it as their personal scoop. I smiled and considered it personal flattery.

CHAPTER 6

How News Gets Born

Today, more than fifty years after I started in the business, people still ask the same question, "How do you get the stories?"

The answer is "Good team work by staff, organization and planning ahead, and reliance on the Day Book, still in use on every city desk." It reminds the desk man of all coming trials, executions, interviews and utility rate hearings, down to the almost newsless luncheon meeting of a few small clubs. Luck and happenstance, then and today, played on insignificant part in bringing home an exclusive story.

The paper prided itself on covering all sources of news about town. Major fires were bold headlines, in the mid-fifties, like the enormous play they get today from TV channels. Every newspaper office had an alarm box ticker that printed on tape the location of all fires, including the number of alarms and calls for special equipment. Single alarms in the business and shopping areas were covered, while the outlying districts only received attention when the fire grew to a multi-alarm blaze. The town was covered by beats with reporters, stationed at various public buildings, sometimes called "listening posts."

Two men were assigned to City Hall exclusively while others drew duty at the Public Utilities and State building across the street and the Federal Courts in the old Post Office.

One of the most important and highest paid beat men was the police reporter, always on call at the ancient Hall of Justice on Kearny Street. The police felt so secure in their fortress that no locks were ever provided in the original plans for the main doors. Beat men liked being assigned there because of its proximity to Chinatown with its numerous selection of good cafes.

From the time of the Gold Rush in 1849, San Francisco Bay was the major maritime port on the

Pacific Coast. The gradual decline set in following the Vietnam conflict. It seemed forever that every type of vessel was seen riding the waters off the Embarcadero, and now it feels like only moments ago. Many of the major lines left the Bay and others have gone out of business.

The shipping editor is gone, along with the special shipping columns and news sections that appealed to subscribers. The ship beat man was responsible not only for all arriving vessels and the VIP passengers aboard, but for most departing steamers too, their cargo and ports of destination.

When a San Francisco bound luxury liner hove to off the Farralones, prior to entering port, the Bar Pilot launch responded. They would put a veteran skipper aboard to steer the ship through the treacherous tides, rocks and shoals outside the gate. The pilot boat usually went out at five in the morning and the shipping editor "better be aboard."

The frightening part of the trip occurred when the tiny pilot boat came alongside the giant liner. The reporter had to time the swells perfectly, jump out and grab the heaving Jacobs ladder and scamper up more than sixty feet to the main deck above.

I had that thrill, once was enough. When our shipping editor took a busman's holiday cruise to the South Sea Islands, I took off too.

At topside the purser handed out a list of prominent people aboard and while the liner was slowly heading in and docking, the press had ample time for interviews. After the liner tied up and the phone lines to shore were connected, the reporter dictated his story to a secretary on the city desk. The most enjoyable part of the beat came when the interview work was finished. The Captain would then treat the press to a luxury breakfast in the main dining salon. The only directive was, "...order anything you want."

CHAPTER 7

Central Emergency, A Most Important Beat

During my reporting days the press room at Central Emergency Hospital in Civic Center was considered of such news importance that it was never left uncovered during print hours. The room was the size of a closet with no windows or ventilation and located next to the operating room, with all its howls of pain and fright. Fresh air came in only when the door was left ajar.

Most editors considered the rooms a good training ground for cub members of the staff and since I was still a rookie, I drew that assignment for almost a year. Countless page one stories were "born" there and the rookies acknowledged the place as being equal to a class in news reporting. Little stories, originating there, often developed into big headliners.

Today the little room is usually empty, the beat uncovered and visited only occasionally by a passing reporter, stopping to use a free phone.

The late Dr. Jacob "Jake" Geiger was Director of Public Health and had offices upstairs over Central Emergency in the Health Building. He was a wonderful friend, a buddy to the press with a phone line always open and available, day or night.

If any news was withheld at San Francisco Hospital or any of the city's five emergency hospitals, ambulance crews refused to cooperate and blocked a good action picture, a quick phone call to "Jake" instantly solved the problem.

He was also sympathetic in helping reporters with a drinking problem get "dried out" at the hospital. No questions were asked and the reporter's name never showed on the entry log book.

Dr. Geiger became such as friend that when I got married at Stanford Chapel a couple of years later, he drove to Palo Alto in an April rain shower to wish me luck.

Some of the stories I gathered at the emergency were so unbelievable and haunting they give me the shudders I feel now while writing this horror. Even editors found some of the stories so incredible they would phone the press room to question the facts.

One of the bad days was the morning a well-dressed middle aged woman walked in to the emergency clutching a bloody bath towel to her chest. On it was dressmaking shears and the major portion of her tongue. She handed the chief steward a scribbled note that said, "My husband always calls me a nag with a big tongue, so I got rid of it." She fainted and I felt sick.

Every type of accident eventually showed up in the treatment room. The broiled roofer was next. Before the war, roofing trucks would haul open kettles of near boiling tar on trailers attached to their trucks. At the job site the roofer would hop off the rear of the truck and start on the job. This unlucky day his foot caught in the tail gate slot in the bed of the truck and he went tumbling and screaming, head first, into the pot of tar. His crew pulled him out and rushed him to Central. Nothing could be done...only pronounce him dead.

A similar accident happened on Harrison Street south of Market in a zinc coating works. Fire escapes and other heavy metal objects that needed plating to become rust resistant, were dipped into a well of molten zinc, set level with the floor. A crane did the dipping and the lifting out. No safety railings were in place to avoid against accidents. Again, a worker slipped or tripped into the zinc bath. When the crane managed to hook and lift him out, he was beyond recognition, a glistening skeleton.

CHAPTER 8

The Sidewalk Question Man

When I entered the business, The Question Man column was already a popular feature, the same as today, and occupied a spot of recognition on the section page. The "question," usually one of national interest or the hot topic of local controversy, was selected by George West, our top editorial writer.

The inquiring reporter would pick a sidewalk station at a busy corner downtown, most often Fifth and Market and tried to carry on a conversation with the first six pedestrians to stop. Many couldn't be bothered and kept on walking.

"This is going to be good experience for you," Sontheimer explained. "Phone interviews are no cinch, but stopping people in the street and getting them to talk is something else, needing great charm." How right he was.

The first columns were not easy. People thought I was selling something and kept walking. Others asked, "What will you pay for my answer?" Any stage fright left in the reporter was soon lost. Many answers were in such poor shape, with incomplete English and faulty syntax, that a rewrite job had to be done back at the office.

CHAPTER 9

Walking The G. G. Bridge Catwalk

Two of the most important local stories, warranting almost daily news coverage and photos, were the start of construction on the Golden Gate and Bay Bridges in 1935.

The public, clamoring for ties to Marin and the East Bay since the days following the gold rush, showed tremendous interest in the projects. They were getting, not only one, but two spans of world record-breaking proportions.

Work went on around the clock as did the press coverage whenever a most hazardous or spectacular phase of construction was being performed. Erection of the twin towers and the spinning of the steel cable attracted the most attention.

The cables that would support the bridge roadway were huge and too long for installation in one piece. They were strung in single strands, one at a time, as a spider would spin a web. One strand of cable, the thickness of a lead pencil, was fabricated from case hardened chrome steel.

When the first strands were in place and adjusted to proper tension and camber, the workers hung a wooden catwalk, the width of a dining table under the cables to be used as a workspace and inspection platform.

No part of the bridge roadway was yet in place, that would come months later, and all the while the spinning wheel kept up the monotonous pace, back and forth, day and night.

The workers showed not the slightest fear of the tremendous heights and clamored about the towers and cables like squirrels in their favorite tree. Their scrambling looked so easy until I tried it later. How wrong I was. I found out the hard way when I was asked to take that stroll over the Golden Gate.

It came about most casually. The boss stopped by my desk and suggested, "What about a feature story on crossing the catwalk? It would be a natural and

Muller was the first civilian to ride the the construction engine across the Bay Bridge before it opened in 1938.

you'd be the first reporter to pull off the stunt."
Many afternoons my wife and I had parked atop the
Presidio Hills and watched the spinning of the
cables. We saw no danger or possible fright;
apparently our view was much too distant.

Never giving it a second thought, I said, "Sure,"
and took off for the bridge wearing slacks and jacket,
no windproof overalls or nonslip boots and much
needed goggles. I was most unprepared.

The crew foreman met me at the construction
shack and took me by elevator to the top of the
South (San Francisco) tower and led me by the hand
past the giant saddle that would hold the finished
cable in place, then on to the catwalk itself.

I would be walking down to the center of the span
and it wasn't too frightening...yet. "Don't ever look
down," he directed..."That's the worst thing you could
do. I'll be here when you get back."

I didn't feel too nervous and felt I could make
it...that was...until I started the climb up the steep
grade to the North tower (Marin). The wind, without
warning, kicked up with the slap of a hundred whips.
The catwalk trembled and so did I. The easy stroll I
had hoped for and had been expecting turned into a
frightening reality. My instincts for survival
overcame me and I sunk to my hands and knees and
finished the ordeal in a baby crawl.

One thought was on my mind, "Get me off this
damned bridge." My slacks were ruined and that
didn't matter, for I'd have given my whole suit and
everything else I had to "Get the hell out of there." I
believe it was a miracle, for atop the Marin tower a
worker, watching my antics, hurried over to give me
a saving arm tow and hustled me to the base of the
tower.

"How are you gonna get back, kid?" he asked.

"The only safe way, by ferryboat."

Back at the office the staff gathered around to ask
"How it felt." I'd never confess my fears to them;
tried to play it cool and replied..."Great, wasn't scary
at all. I loved the view." I went to my desk and
wrote, "On Ribbons of Steel I Crossed the Golden Gate
Today."

Under my story was an editor's box pointing out I

was the first reporter, or civilian to cross the cat.

Several years later while the Bay Bridge was nearing completion and the steel rails to carry Southern Pacific and Key system electric trains were being spiked into place on the lower deck, I had a similar first. This one I enjoyed. I hand pumped a construction car across the bay to San Francisco. It was a "piece of cake," nothing like the Gate story.

CHAPTER 10

Meeting The President

Many people have always admired the lifestyle of newspapermen and have declared, sometimes with admiration or even envy, "You must meet the most interesting people." I did. When I wrote this chapter I counted back to list all of the American Presidents I have met and interviewed, from President Roosevelt through Ronald Reagan, nine in all.

The list of characters, famous and infamous, was endless and included every local judge up the Supreme Court level, politicians, business men and con men, prostitutes, law men and VIPS and even the youngest shoe shine boy in the lobby at the Hall of Justice. They all helped to fill the daily pages.

Meeting or even catching a glimpse of former President Herbert Hoover never came my way and no way can I consider it a personal loss.

During the summer of 1930 my parents were out of town on vacation and rather than playing house sitting in San Francisco, I enrolled in a couple of classes in summer school at Stanford.

Hoover had just been nominated for president by the Republican Convention and was heading west to his San Juan Hill home on the campus to rest for the fall campaign.

When it was learned that Mr. Hoover would arrive in Palo Alto on a special train at seven that evening, the students quickly organized a rally committee, formed a torch light parade, and led by the hand, proudly marched to Palo Alto depot to welcome him home. We were puffed with pride, feeling sure that a Stanford man, one of us, was going to be the next President.

When the train stopped, Mr. Hoover pulled, what we thought to be a most discourteous political act; he alighted on the opposite side of the track, hopped into his limousine, shades down, and took off at high speed for his home. Still undaunted, we hiked up the hill and started a bigger rally outside his front walk. The songs were louder and so were the school yells.

The drapes in the house were drawn tight and there wasn't a peek or peep from Mr. Hoover. At the very least we expected a hand wave. Nothing, not a sign of life from the home. Our noise went on for fifteen minutes. Possibly as a way of getting rid of us, Mrs. Hoover opened the front door, halfway and announced, "Thanks for coming. Mr. Hoover is tired and needs to rest." That was all and she was gone.

I had feelings of disgust and rejection as I marched down the hill with the other students to the library.

President Harry Truman was the complete opposite in personality. He was ever at ease in communicating with people and his relations with the members of the press were of the best.

Whenever he came to town he would stay at the Fairmont Hotel and always invite the press along on his well remembered walks atop Nob Hill. He was most considerate of the needs of the press and gave special orders to his aides to be sure his Secret Service agents did not relegate any reporters to a position in the rear of the pack. Questions were answered freely and completely and a "No Comment" was seldom heard.

One morning I was returning to the office from a Truman walk and was called to cover a murder in the heart of skid row. A known prostitute was found sprawled nude in the rear of a parking lot, stabbed to death, her genital organs cut out and stuffed in her throat. This bit of horror was not included for shock appeal, no, only to show how the people and the social level of assignments dipped from exclusive Nob Hill to the dregs of the Tenderloin.

Ronald Reagan, with his hearty friendliness was one of my favorites. Other news people, especially the ladies, felt the same. I first met him when he was sitting in Sacramento as governor.

A suite of offices was set aside for him on the top floor of the State Building in the Civic Center and, on the few occasions he visited San Francisco, his secretary called all news sources to announce a press conference. The sessions were almost a carbon copy of the press meetings he held years later in the White House. The meetings were pleasant occasions, not due only to his personal charm but also to a special invitation to a splendid lunch at the Pacific Union Club on Nob Hill. The grilled French lamb chops were four inches thick, by measurement.

Back in his Sacramento days, President Reagan first started making you feel proud you were an American.

CHAPTER 11

San Jose Lynching

My first major murder case, climaxed by a lynching, was a slaying of Brook Hart in San Jose. The horror and dramatic ending of the kidnapping was so unexpected it pushed the affair into national attention in a single night, made banner headlines in every paper and stunned California and the nation. The year was 1932.

Lynch justice was thought to have been ended in the last days of the Vigilantes in California, and now, more than a half century later, mob rule was back in power, leading a gang of ten thousand screaming people. Looking back, it was later estimated that while only fifty men planned and led the lynching, no power on earth could have stopped that army from reaping its vengeance.

Young Hart, 22, handsome and popular, was the only son of the prominent family that owned Hart's Department store in downtown San Jose. He was snatched on the sidewalk the afternoon of November ninth near his father's store by two local hoodlums, Thomas Thurmond and John Holmes. They were a few years older than their victims, unemployed and broke and thought the snatch an easy way to pick up $40,000 in ransom money.

Brooke was bound, gagged and spirited to an old shack, near the town of Milpitas. He was forced to write two ransom notes to his parents, giving no time for a reply and then was brutally murdered.

The family insisted on knowing if their son was alive and demanded snapshots of the boy before proceeding with any ransom negotiations. The kidnappers were so callous about the affair they wired the already dead youth's eyes open with piano wire, took pictures and sent them to the family. The photos were so out of focus the family readily accepted them as genuine.

Police got their first break several days later when Brook's wallet that had been tossed into the South Bay was found settled on the gunwale (wooden side rail of a ship) of an anchored vessel. Further bungled ransom attempts followed and eventually led to the arrest of the pair.

They were taken to the old red brick county jail across the street from St. James Park. Hart's body was found floating in the bay next to the San Mateo Bridge on November 22nd.

At that time San Jose was a small town of fruit orchards, truck gardens and farm machinery plants. Work spread quickly about the finding of the body and a crowd started gathering outside the jail.

The time was Sunday afternoon, (following the Stanford-California Game and I was home, resting up from the celebration of the night before.) Fortunately, I was home when City Editor Sontheimer called explaining the situation in San Jose and the rumor of a possible lynching.

He said it would be an all night assignment and even if nothing happened, I was to get full overtime. I wasn't too happy but I went and stationed myself in front of the jail and mingled with other reporters whose editors had received the same rumor. No radio persons were present and television was way in the future. When dusk arrived and nothing had happened, most of the press left the scene to get dinner uptown. I had already eaten at home so I stayed behind. Therefore a major portion of the press corps was eating and not present to witness the start of the grisly drama.

The first ranks of the mob started to arrive, spurred on by too much drinking and began spraying doors of the jail with rocks and insults. Nearby was an unlimited supply of hurling and battering material for the crowd.

The new County Court House was under construction next door and the builders had stacked a load of heavy steel water pipes that were to be used

Brooke Hart

hn Holmes

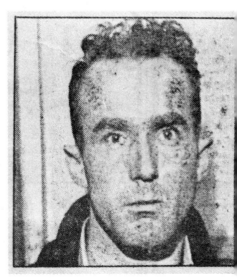

Thomas Thurmond

to supply the fire extinguisher systems being built into the structure. The pipes were heavy and long enough to make ideal battering rams, capable of smashing open the doors of any jail. The horror, that was to last three hours, had started.

A public phone booth luckily left behind from a recently concluded murder trial, was standing empty about 100 feet from the main doors of the jail. I took it over and kept that phone hot for the next few hours.

My paper didn't go to press until the next day but I knew I was responsible for getting the story to our national wire service. My booth was the closest to the action. Our City Editor Sontheimer was dining at the home of Dick Chase, his assistant, and while the smashing and gassing was going on I delivered a play by play report to Chase. His wife told me later he was so excited in talking over his wall phone that he scribbled parts of my story across one whole wall in the family dining room.

The defenders inside the jail put up a good fight but later their zeal began to cool and instead of dropping their tear gas bombs on the heads of the mob battering below at the doors, the police, with token resistance, lofted the shells over the heads of the attackers; the gas made direct hits on my phone booth. Finally the doors were breached and the shelling stopped. I left the booth to escape the gas and get a better view of the scene and found myself helpless when the mob surged forward in a wave and swept me inside the jail.

All was violence, gas fumes and curses. The law men knew they were outnumbered and readily stepped aside while the mob pulled the shocked prisoners from their cells and dragged them, sometimes by the hair, into St. James Park.

The nooses were already hanging from an oak tree and while some of the mob adjusted the ropes, others behaving like wild animals, tore off the clothes of the kidnappers, who, struck dumb with fear never uttered a sound.

The mob was not yet satisfied. While the victims slowly revolved in the breeze, some made torches from rolled newspapers and set fire to the dead men's genitals. Some fathers hoisted their young children to their shoulders to give them a better look at the horror.

Later I went to the Saint Clair Hotel and wrote my story. My cameraman had taken a wide range photo of the break in and his picture, unknown to me, showed me in action in the phone booth. The photo was splashed across the front page and our artist painted in white arrows to show my exclusive vantage post.

A national roar of revulsion swept across the country in the days that followed. Governor James "Sunny Jim" Rolph praised the mob and declared, "Send your kidnappers to California, we know how to take care of them," and added, "I'll pardon any member of the mob that is arrested." President Franklin Roosevelt and most national leaders expressed revulsion and shame.

Newsman Arthur Brisbane, chief editorial writer for the Hearst papers, summed up the horrible event in his TODAY column with, "A mob can break into your home, a mob can break into your Sacramento Capitol and a mob can break into your Treasury in Washington. You have no defense."

Chronicle reporter Royce Brier went to San Jose the next day, checked all sources, even talked to some of the mob and wrote a masterful story that won him the Pulitzer Prize.

I was still a green cub, thinking that somewhere, a national editorial board made the prize selection. I never knew then that the reporter himself had to submit his own nomination.

CHAPTER 12

Captain Ahab

Following the howling nightmare of the San Jose lynching drama, my paper, the San Francisco News, promoted Richard Chase to the post of City Editor. He was a likeable young man with a keen interest in illustrated feature stories.

He believed that fantasy feature stories on expeditions led by Capt. Ahab, the legendary whale hunter, surrounded by a bevy of beautiful young girls were gags the readers would appreciate. He was one of the first to advocate leg art, then called cheesecake.

The part of Capt. Ahab the intrepid leader was assigned to me, possibly because of my age and height, (I was six foot three.) The supporting female crew members, with never the same girl featured twice, were selected from the several charm schools in the downtown area. The charm colleges were glad to cooperate when they learned it meant a credit line for their school under our news pictures.

My uniform, usually the same costume, was an admirable full length blue coat with ridiculous floppy gold epaulets and, of course, an ornate sword. Topping all was an admiral's hat, sometimes plumed, with braided visors fore and aft. My biggest problem was mastering my wooden peg leg. It took some doing just to stand upright on shore.

Later the trick was to keep from tumbling into the bay from the stern of a battered old life boat which we borrowed from the Harbor Master.

Chase insisted every sea going expedition should have its own bartender aboard to care for all the tippling. We took along Schmaltz, who used to slide 'em down the mahogany plank at the corner bar. The first mate on our fictitious cruises was gorgeous Zoe Dell Lantis, theme girl of the 1939 fair on Treasure Island. We called her the "Eye Stopper." Her garb was a skimpy pirate outfit, considered quite shocking in those days but probably overdressed today. Her role

Captain Ahab (Baron Muller) and Zoe Dell Landis, theme girl of the 1939 World's Fair, searching for whale in San Francisco Bay. Serving grog is Schmaltz.

was to attract nationwide visitors to the fair, and she did.

Meanwhile, a young sperm whale drifted into the bay, became disoriented and was spotted thrashing around in the deep water off Alcatraz Island. Public interest was high but nothing to equal delight of our city editor. Every ferry boat skipper spotted the creature and the event was kept alive for days.

The Capt. Ahab forces including the lovely Zoe Dell and Schmaltz of course, were mobilized and ordered to sea to find the whale. The prize was never spotted, but that didn't matter too much since nobody fell overboard. The story was funny and the pictures so unique they were printed oversize.

Early this Spring, exposition officials celebrated a fifty year reunion on Treasure Island for all who had participated in the fair. Zoe Dell flew in from Indiana and surprised everyone by slipping into the identical pirate garb she wore a half a century ago. It was no tight squeeze.

Always on the watch for an unusual situation, Chase had the Ahab players busy on the streets almost monthly. One of the silliest happenings for a photo story was the breakdown of the cable cars serving Nob Hill, putting the line out of service for days. Chase phantasied the residents atop the hill as being stranded and without food.

Chase thought it would be amusing to have Capt. Ahab set up a horse meat stand near Grace Cathedral and pretend to sell meat to the hungry and stranded citizens. A well trained mare was borrowed from the mounted police patrol, aprons, cooks hats and butcher equipment from the Fairmont Hotel and the "rescue" operation was in business. Crowds always gathered at these stunts, many imagining a movie sequence was being filmed.

Before the underground Union Square Garage, across from the St. Francis Hotel opened to the public, the Ahab team was marshalled for a land operation. The gig was to determine if the air in the deeper levels was safe. We were told to act like coal miners and do the testing with caged canaries.

The captain and his girls borrowed caged birds from Robinson's Pet Shop and put on a fun show. deep in the bowels of the garage. Not a bird was lost.

Muller, a friend and the canary. All three survived.

CHAPTER 13

The Frank Egan Case
(Solved Three Months Before It
Happened)

The Frank Egan Murder case, solved three months before it happened, occurred about the same time as the San Jose lynching. It gave the city its second dose of national press attention.

I didn't cover the case from its inception, nor did I hear most of the presentation of the unbelievable evidence. I did do a modest amount of work before the matter went to the jury. Veteran police reporters at the Hall of Justice filled me with all the evidence, hoping to get a reaction of horror. They did.

Frank Egan had the distinction of being the city's first Public Defender and also the first in the State of California. He was a natural for the newly created post. Tall and handsome, a native son, Irish of course, a former policeman who bettered himself by going into law, via night school classes. He was a man with countless friends.

Within the next few years success came too easy and fast for him. His new lifestyle of high living was slowly pushing him into debts that were getting ever harder to pay. Only money could get him out of his troubles, and that money would be easy pickings with the death of Mrs. Jessie Scott Hughes, a wealthy widow and long time doting client.

At this time, the early 30's, there were no exclusive medical buildings yet built. Doctors and dentists treated patients in the parlors of their homes or took offices in the downtown Phelan and Flood buildings.

Here we meet Dr. Nathan Houseman, a well known surgeon, suspected of being unethical and under suspicion by the police. He had offices in the Flood Building, at Powell and Market street and a complete miniature hospital in adjoining rooms. Police were told the hospital was always open to any of the doctor's patients, victims of a holdup or shooting. A wanted criminal need only crawl to Dr. Houseman's safe haven, have his wounds treated and convalesce until the "heat was off."

The police were unable to secure presentable legal evidence against the doctor, evidence they felt would be strong enough to present to a grand jury. They apparently became frustrated and planted a bug in the doctor's private office. The listening wires led to the furnace room in the basement. Under orders of Captain of Inspectors Charles W. Dullea, a team of specially selected inspectors did the listening.

The bug was manned only during office hours and every bit of controversy was recorded in shorthand. Defender Egan went about his daily tasks, highly respected, suspected of nothing and had a spotless reputation like Caesars' wife..."above reproach."

Then the "bug" caught its biggest prize. The surprised inspectors knew instantly who it was when Egan walked in and the doctor called out, "Welcome Frank Egan, what can I do for you?"

While the police couldn't believe what they were hearing, Egan went on to tell of his financial difficulties and calmly asked the doctor for, "Medical advise on the best way to kill his wealthy client, Mrs. Hughes."

In an equally calm manner, Dr. Houseman explained the murder plan as follows:

"Set up a perfect alibi for yourself. Set the kill for a Friday night; attend the fights at Dreamland Auditorium and sit at ringside. Make as much noise as possible, that way people will remember you. Holler across the ring to an imaginary friend, ask the time, setting the time alibi."

"Above all, don't go near the Hughes home, but send some of your bully boys you can trust, (ex-cons Egans has sprung in past years). Phone and tell her you are sending some of your boys with a special present, and she should open her garage doors and let them drive in.

"Don't use your own automobile, fingerprints may show up later, but borrow a heavy touring car. Once inside the garage, have them punch her in the belly, throw her on the concrete floor and drive the car over her until she is dead."

"Put a coat on her and dump the body several blocks from home, making it look like the typical hit and run accident." No date was set. The bully boys were Vern Doran and Albert Tinnen, so beholden to Egan they followed the plan without question.

When the murder recordings were given to Capt. Dullea, he immediately put a round-the-clock watch on the home and warned Mrs. Hughes about the plot to kill her for her money.

She wouldn't believe any part of it and dismissed the matter as some fantastic dream. "Frank Egan is my dear friend and lawyer," she insisted. "He would never let anything happen to me."

Since bugging was illegal and Frank Egan so politically powerful, the police never approached him. But they took every possible precaution to protect her, even going to Mrs. Hughes' banker, Parker Maddox, President of the San Francisco bank to get his cooperation to report any withdrawals from her accounts.

Weeks passed. When nothing happened, police imagined Egan and Dr. Houseman possibly knew about the bug and were having a joke, or the plotters had a change of heart and dropped the plan as too risky. Within three months the house watch was removed.

Then it happened. Mrs. Hughes' body was found in the street, as it had been planned with police regarding her as a hit-and-run victim while out for a walk. Suspicion arose when no purse was found at the scene. Police wondered how the little old lady could get back in her home without a purse, door keys or any identification.

Deputy Coroner Mike Brown deepened the mystery when he undressed the body in the morgue. There were no tire marks across the chest and stomach of her cloth coat, but her flower print house coat, worn underneath was ripped and had a series of heavy tire prints. Her fingerprints were sent to Washington and she laid in the morgue, a Jane Doe.

Ten days later word came back that she was

Frank Egan on the witness stand at his trial.

Jessie Scott Hughes. Capt. Dullea started a frenzied manhunt for Egan. Hours later Egan called the captain from a pay phone outside the Ferry Building to erroneously report he was being kidnapped. Before he could tell more the phone went dead. He was trying to make the police believe his abductors had snatched the receiver from his hand. The manhunt went on and not a word leaked about the bugged conversation.

Days later, Attorney Vincent Hallinan, a young lawyer on his first major case, called police and surrendered Egan. The boys, Doran and Tinnen were picked up the same day.

The case tried before Superior Judge Frank Dunne at the old Hall of Justice on Kearny Street turned into a legal hippodrome. Young Hallinan did a masterful job. He objected violently to most questions from the D.A. and presented for the first time his defense tactic..."When you have a weak case, put the cops on trial." In addition he tried to take the jury's minds from the evidence by constantly wrangling with exasperated Judge Dunne who almost daily held Hallinan in contempt of court, setting new records at the Hall.

Hallinan's legal tactics worked so well the jury, to the surprise of all courtroom observers, withheld the death penalty and gave Egan life. Doran, who had earlier turned state's evidence was spared a jail term. Tinnen, regarded as a stupid dupe, received a lesser sentence. Egan served twenty-five years, came out of San Quentin a broken man and died a few months later. While Hallinan was considering filing a motion for a new trial, the Examiner, leading morning paper, broke the exclusive story on the bug in the doctor's office. The drama that resulted was the high point of the case.

While Attorney Hallinan says, "I'm glad I didn't appeal...the notes from the bug would have shown a planned and deliberate cold blooded murder...Egan for sure would have gotten the death penalty."

Captain Dullea later became Chief of Police and his son, Monsignor Charles Dullea, rose to head the University of San Francisco as president.

What about Dr. Houseman? He was investigated by the State Board of Medical Examiners, found guilty of malpractice and the issuance of fraudulent prescriptions and barred from practice for life.

After nearly sixty years of practice, and one of the city's brightest legal minds, Attorney Hallinan is as sharp as ever. His son, Terrance, also a lawyer, is a member of the San Francisco Board of Supervisors.

CHAPTER 14

April Aaron:
Senseless Violence Hits the
Streets

Following the San Jose night of horror, I advanced from the rating of cub and was considered a veteran, possibly due to my baptism of tear gas. Now I was being assigned to every kind of crime as it happened.

Many newsmen, writing their memoirs, told how they covered the major stories. They called them the "big ones." I'm so proud to report that I covered the "little ones" too. Somebody had to cover them and no one ever knew when the little items would develop into the top stories.

One such was the April Aaron story. The date was April 18, 1962. Police consider it the start of senseless cuttings and violence that followed, in a city that had its share of crime, but without the viciousness of maiming for no apparent reason.

April, a pretty twenty-two-year-old secretary, was living at home with her parents in the vicinity of Golden Gate Park. She enjoyed walking the area after dinner and the evening hours held no fears for her. No one had ever bothered her. On the night in question, she walked alone to attend a social supper and dance at her church in the nearby area. The evening was pleasant. She danced and chatted with friends, had a happy time and left for home around ten pm, a conservative hour, she thought.

While she was still in sight of her church, she heard footsteps and turned to see someone following her. She started running through the park and her attacker ran faster, grabbing her near the rhododendron bushes and throwing her to the earth.

He grabbed her purse and began rummaging for money and other valuables. She believed he was only after her cash, no harm would happen and she didn't need to put up a fight or scream. Apparently angered by not finding a thing of value, her assailant, without a word, reached into his coat, pulled out a boning knife and slashed her across the face with one giant swipe. The blow severed her right eye. Still not sated, he bent down and hacked her across the left wrist with cuts so deep the tendons were shredded and the wrist forever useless.

In a final burst of anger he cut her across the right thigh so furiously that doctors at Mission Emergency Hospital first thought they would have to amputate the leg. They were able to save the limb buy not the sight of the right eye or the use of the left wrist. Her assailant, apparently satisfied, took off and was never found.

April screamed and fainted and was later found by police who first thought she was dead. Crime files marked that Spring night as the start of all senseless personal attacks.

CHAPTER 15

Khrushchev Comes To Town

Local television channels caught up with the print media in popularity and news appeal during the official visit here of the Soviet leader Nikita Khrushchev. The date was September, 1959. It was a special invitation from Mayor George Christopher.

Khrushchev insisted he wanted to see first hand how the American people lived, worked and even played during a typical day. He wanted to learn how our school classes were taught and to spend some time in an average San Francisco home, visiting the family and perhaps even eating dinner with them.

Chief of Police, Thomas J. Cahill, aware that this type of informal touring could create security problems, tried to minimize the guarding issue by surrounding Khrushchev with a hand-picked squad of police detectives. All stood over six foot. Reporters surmised that Chief Cahill picked his tallest men just to make the tiny visitor more conscious of his short stature.

They towered so completely that wherever the official party toured, Khrushchev could not be seen beyond a few feet. Trailing along in the rear, of course, was a body guard of Soviet secret police, all wearing bulky overcoats to hide the automatic weapons they had slung under their armpits.

Eventually Khrushchev visited every place he had requested, with the exception of his fondest wish: to visit Disneyland. The State Department nixed that trip as too much of a security risk.

A few days before the Soviet party arrived, police were swamped with countless requests for press cards, police badges and special identification to get through the police lines. Chief Cahill called a press conference in the police auditorium atop the Hall of Justice. Every press official and TV anchor person was invited. Harry Press, my city editor was unable to attend the huddle and asked me to represent him.

Chairing the conference was Captain John Butler,

Department Secretary. He spelled out what we could do, what to expect and how to conduct ourselves. When he finished setting the ground rules, he put the same question to all in the assembly, "What are your special needs?" Instead of calling upon the written press first, as was always the practice in the past, he turned, recognized the representative from Channel 5 and asked for their specific needs. That hit me hard and for the first time I realized our days as the exclusive ink press were numbered. We were starting to play "second fiddle" to the TV news gatherers.

Nikita Krushchev at the Mark Hopkins Hotel, September 21, 1959. Police Chief Tom Cahill is in the background, left.

CHAPTER 16

Executions At San Quentin

I was on the staff three years before I witnessed my first execution in San Quentin Prison across the bay in Marin County. I felt that education as a street smart reporter would never be complete until I had witnessed a legal death.

Whenever I learned of an upcoming hanging, I would pester the city editor for the assignment. The answer was always the same, "You're still too green...you need more experience...have patience."

My chance came sooner that I expected. Two weeks later the boss called and said, "You've got it. There's a hanging at Quentin tomorrow. Do a good job and don't get sick till after you phone in the story." On the drive over to the prison I kept asking myself how I would possibly react to the horror I was about to witness.

A stern looking guard with a clip board listing all the names of witnesses, checked me in at the front gate. In addition to my press card, I had to show special credentials that were issued for that day. Reporters and witnesses were led into a huge barn-like loft on the fourth floor that once had served as a factory for the manufacture of wooden door frames and window blinds. In the center of the hall stood the gallows, made of heavy wooden beams, painted a pale prison gray with 13 steps leading up to the spot where the condemned dropped into eternity. Two trap doors, to enable a pair to be hung together, were built into the floor of the gallows.

The traps, much wider that a human body, had black marks painted in the center to show the guards where the condemned person was to stand.

The triggering mechanism was a spring located under the floor of the gallows with three release cords attached to the bottom of each trap door. The cords in turn led to the top of a heavy wooden table and were stretched taut like the strings on a musical instrument. Three guards sat at the table, each with a butcher knife, ready to cut his cord at a signal from the warden. Only one cord was activated, the other two were dummies. The guards never knew which knife had sprung the trap. Deep furrows had been gouged into the table from the cord cuttings of 194 hangings that first started in 1893.

I gathered at the foot of the gallows with other reporters and official witnesses while the warden gave a signal to bring in the prisoner, a southern California hoodlum convicted of murdering a shop keeper in cold blood.

Two guards, each with a hand under the man's armpits, hustled him up the 13 steps, stood him on

The gas chamber at San Quentin.

the painted spot. After the noose and a black bag that had been placed over his head were adjusted, the trapdoor was sprung. It dropped with a horrible bang and the hanged man swung round and round like a punching dummy. The prison doctor then stepped forward and put a football tackle on the swinging body. Next, he tore open the shirt to use his stethoscope to listen for his heart beat. Minutes later he turned and announced, "I declare the prisoner dead," and gave his official time.

That was all. My curiosity had been satisfied and I felt no feelings of revulsion, only numbness. One sensation remained with me for months. That loft had the terrible scent of fear and death, the same foul smell given off by injured wild animals.

The year 1938 marked the end of the hated gallows in San Quentin Prison. Local and national opponents of "The Rope," had annoyed the state legislature for years with phone calls, wires and letters, labeling the gallows as "most cruel and inhuman," and demanding its removal. Banner carrying demonstrators marched and screamed outside the main gate of the prison days prior to a hanging, and at night carried on the same crusade with a parade lighted by candles in glass jars.

The legislature following long and spirited debates, caved in to public pressure, abolished hanging and ordered a lethal gas chamber from an eastern manufacturer., The inmates quickly dubbed it "The Room of Death." I had never seen anything more grim.

It was an eight sided steel cylinder, the size of a large wine vat, with panes of safety glass on the upper half of all sides, giving the witness an unobstructed view of the execution. To handle a double gassing, two metal arm chairs are bolted to the floor in the center of the chamber. Leather restraint straps dangle from the arm rests and the chairs have a row of large holes drilled into the seats to enable the rising cyanide gas to reach the condemned man more quickly.

The killing mechanism is rather simple. Cement bowls, resembling soup tureens and filled with sulfuric acid, are built into the concrete floor under each chair. Long metal rods, hinged to the bottom of each chair and suspended inches above the bowls, hold cloth sacks of cyanide pellets. The other end of the rod passes through the outer shell of the chamber and is fitted with a turning knob at the end. At a sign from the warden, a guard quickly flips the knob, dipping the sack of pellets into the acid. Deadly gas forms instantly and death is less than minutes away.

The chamber, a most gruesome tank to view for the first time, or any other time, fills the center of a large room adjoining the death row cells on the first floor. Like the gallows, there is ample viewing room on all sides for official witnesses and spectators. For some unknown reason it is painted a pale apple green, giving it a most unlikely appearance. The door, a narrow slit and barely wide enough for a man to pass through, resembles a hatchway in a submarine compartment. It is made airtight by screwing tight dog bolts on each side. A large chimney and fan in the ceiling, extends thirty feet into the outside air to dispose of the deadly gas following an execution.

At the designated hour of execution, the prisoner is brought from his cell and strapped into one of the chairs. Next, the prison doctor attaches a stethoscope with a long trailing rubber tube to the prisoner's heart by adhesive tape. The other end of the tube is passed from the chamber through an airtight connection to a table where the warden and doctor will be observing.

When the knob is turned and the pellets drop into the bowl of acid, a low hissing sound comes through the glass panels. Most of the spectators shudder. They all know it is the end. Should a last minute reprieve from the governor's office come over the private phone line attached to a nearby wall, there is no possible way for the warden to stop the execution.

In less that two minutes the prisoner's head slumps to his chest, while the doctor, listening from his checkout table, pronounces death and gives the official time. It is hours before the deadly gas is vented and the body released to an undertaker.

Court Smith, Warden at Quentin when the new

The gas chamber from the point of view of the condemned.

gas chamber was installed was an exacting official. Along with the other penal humanists, he insisted the device should first be tested on a live animal, rather than a human. After it was agreed that a pig's lung structure is similar to that of man, it was decided to select a small piggy from the swine herd at the prison farm. The honor of being the first guinea pig went to Solomon, a little fat porker.

The press was invited and I was told to slant the story as if it was the death of a living person. I showed up with our head cameraman, Eddie Murphy, hoping to get some unusual pictures. The warden not only banned Eddie but gave me a lecture on the prison's strict edict against cameras. "It's only a pig," I argued, but that had no effect.

Meanwhile, I didn't object too strenuously because I had already thought of a way to get around the picture ban. I stood at the closest viewing window and jotted down a complete description of Solomon as the guards carried him in a slatted wooden crate and placed him on the armrest between two chairs. Within minutes it was an accomplished fact. Solomon was dead and the new lethal machine was pronounced a success.

I hurried out, told Murphy what we needed and directed him to a hog ranch on the outskirts of nearby San Rafael. Ten bucks made the rancher most cooperative and in minutes he came back from the mud with a twin of Solomon clutched under his arm. He was holding the animal so tightly that our picture resembled the same pained facial expression Solomon showed as he was dying.

Back at the office I pounded out the story, never saying a word about the substitution of victims. There was plenty of space on the front page that day, news was sparse, and Solomon blossomed forth in a four column spread with his mug.

As soon as the home edition was delivered throughout Marin County, Warden Smith called. He wanted to know just how I managed to smuggle a camera into his prison. He was sure it was concealed in my vest or tie. I denied everything and told him, "We never revealed our sources of news." Several months later I met him at the Press Club bar and he was, "still wondering."

My city editor never suspected the switch and I never told him. When he said the picture and story were "Great," that made it great.

During my early years on the staff of The News, I covered five hangings and six gassings and trying all the time to keep my personal thoughts well in the background. Following the outlawing of the gallows, and whenever a scheduled execution date was announced, my fellow staffers and some friends on the police force, would put the same question to me.

"What method of death would you advocate...rope or gas and which is less traumatic?"

Neither. Both ways are horrible. There is no such thing as an easy way to die. However, if I still had to choose between the two evils, it would be hanging. It is the quickest way.

You already know how the prisoner is hustled up the steps of the gallows, positioned on the black mark on the floor and within minutes is swinging into eternity.

Many people who have never seen an execution think that gas chamber is more humane. I regard that as a fallacy. Too many torturous delays are built into the system.

The door to the chamber is naturally narrow and while one guard tries to pull the prisoner through the entrance way, another guard is outside, pushing from the rear. Often the prisoner resists violently, grabs hold of the door jamb and a pushing match ensues, finally settled when a third guard is summoned to push from the rear.

Once he is inside, the prisoner is pushed into one of the metal chairs and the restraining begins, with wide leather straps buckled around the wrist, arms, legs and chest. More time is consumed. Meanwhile the condemned man is staring out the windows, mumbling his prayers or screaming curses at the guards and witnesses.

The doctor comes in next to attach a stethoscope to the man's chest with adhesive tape and makes sure the tube connection to the ear pieces is leak proof. The guards make a final check of the acid bowl and before leaving, advises the prisoner, "Take deep breaths while the gas is rising. That will make it easier on you. Don't fight it."

When the guards step out, there is another final delay while the door is screwed shut, making the chamber air tight. It is my opinion that all this time consuming procedure is subjecting the prisoner to unnecessary horror and torture. He sits strapped and rigid while all eyes at the windows follow his every facial expression.

More horror is yet to come, and often does if the prisoner can hold his breath for minutes. The facial torture is unbelievable. This is the grimmest part of the drama.

The last two executions I covered at Quentin were gassing of the beautiful murderess Barbara Graham and the infamous torturer Carl Chessman. I interviewed Chessman several times while he legally fought for months to stay alive. We became good friends and before he died he asked his attorney to send me an autographed copy of his book.

It was then I realized I had covered enough death. I didn't want to see any more, and I have never returned to the chamber loft.

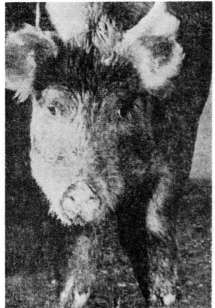

Solomon the pig proved the lethal aspect of the gas chamber.

CHAPTER 17

Baron Meets 'Baron'

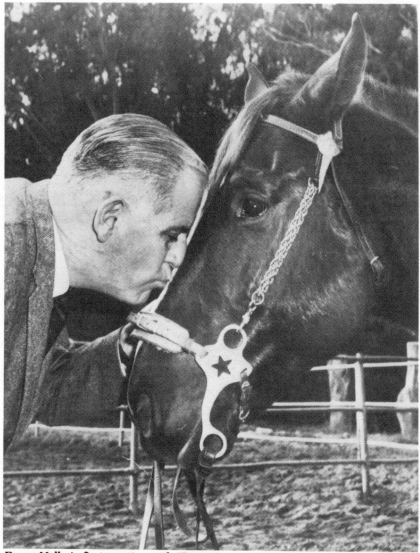

Baron Muller's first meeting with "Baron."

Twenty years ago a bit of unexpected distinction came my way when a young police horse, a magnificent chestnut gelding and the pride of the mounted patrol, was renamed "Baron." I felt doubly honored, since up to that time, no newspaperman had a horse tagged with his name. All of the other animals in the patrol were named for present or former chiefs, or mayors, but never for a reporter.

Chief of Inspectors Martin Lee, a long time friend and the source of many good stories when I covered the police beat, showed his friendship by having the horse named for me. It was flattering indeed, especially when my paper ran a feature story, with a picture of me kissing "Baron" on the forelock. He was a real prize, donated to the department by a local horseman, who later moved to a ranch in Lake County.

Donations by the public were the principal way the police acquired most of their animals, who were all trained for their particular public service in the corrals of the police stables in Golden Gate Park. There they were trained to endure and even ignore every possible city noise and distraction they would face when they were finally assigned to the streets.

Strings of exploding firecrackers were tossed under their hooves, auto horns were blared at them from all sides and tin pails and pot covers were crashed close to their ears.

The final level of training was to ride them at full gallop into the ocean waves below the Cliff House and simulate the rescue of a drowning person. Only a few failed the course. When training was completed, police listed their value at more than ten thousand dollars a head.

I took keen delight in my namesake and rode him through the park several times a month. If I couldn't make a personal visit, I would phone and inquire about his well being.

The morning I called to ask that question, the mounted sergeant shocked me by reporting, "Baron has pneumonia and is down in his stall." "Is it serious?" I want to know. "Oh yes," he answered back, "the virus is such a bad type that it has spread through the entire patrol and all 22 horses are confined to their stalls.

I couldn't believe it and said, "That's a hell of story...big news to anybody."

"Oh, is that news?" he asked. "I didn't know."

"You're damn right it's news. especially since it has never happened here before," I explained and went on to tell him how animal stories have always gone over big in San Francisco.

I did the story and the wire services carried it throughout the country, much to the amazement of the sergeant, who thanked me for his lesson in journalism.

The happy ending is that all of the horses eventually recovered.

CHAPTER 18

The Frenchman Gets His Citizenship

At the end of World War II, so many alien nationals, realizing the benefits of U.S. citizenship, filed their first papers. The overwhelmed Federal Immigration Service selected Superior Court Judge Edmond P. Morgan, hearing civil matters at City Hall to speed along the process. I was covering city hall courts at the time and knew the judge as a good friend of the press, for he liked seeing his name in print.

The principal player in the following drama was Paul Verdier, a dashing Frenchman and buddy of Joseph Cauthorn, then publisher of the San Francisco News. Mr. Verdier owned The City of Paris, the premier fashion store, and was one of our largest advertisers. Mr. Cauthorn always strove to keep him that way.

The best part of the story is told next by Guy Wright, a columnist at the Examiner, who wrote a special story just before I retired from the paper in January, 1979. He titled it, "The One and Only Baron."

Quoting Guy Wright, "One day Mr. Cauthorn called me into his office and said, "My friend Paul Verdier takes his citizenship test tomorrow before Judge Morgan. You know Morgan, make sure Mr. Verdier passes."

"I was flabbergasted," Baron said. E.P. Morgan was bald expect for five hairs that he combed from east to west. We called him Morgan the Magnificent but not within ear shot.

On the bench he was a Captain Bligh. When he spoke of "my court," that's what he meant.

I went to him and explained my predicament, expecting him to explode. Instead he said, "Don't worry Baron. I'll take care of it."

As Baron described the hearing it was a disaster. "What kind of nation is this?", the examiner asked. The Frenchman thought it was a wonderful nation, lovely women, even passable wines but he must have sensed that wasn't what the fellow meant so he said "not a word."

The federal examiner went on to the next question. "How many senators does each state send to Washington?" Verdier knew Washington Senators played that incomprehensible game called baseball, but it never occurred to him to count them. Again Gaelic prudence counseled silence.

After a few similar non-answers the exasperated federal examiner told the judge, "obviously this man should be turned down."

Judge Morgan bristled as much as a man with five hairs can bristle. "This is my court. I make the decisions here," he said. Turning to Verdier he went on, "I'm sure this gentleman knows this is a nation of laws, not men, of government of the people and by the people." He made a little Fourth of July speech and Verdier agreed those were his sentiments.

I'm sure he knows California has two senators. No doubt the Honorable William Knowland and Sheridan Downey are patrons of his fine store. Ah yes, the Frenchman remembered them well. Judge Morgan led him through the catechism and then while the examiner stared speechless, he declared, "I find it an honor to welcome this gentleman as a citizen."

Telling it more than thirty years later, Baron said, "Times have changed, the town has changed. Today there isn't a judge who could pull that off;" "and not a reporter either Baron. We will miss you."

Next day I eagerly awaited a "well done" phone call or memo from publisher Cauthorn. I got neither.

Superior Court Judge George Washington Shonfeld, sitting at City Hall, was also selected to hear naturalization cases when Judge Morgan was unavailable or swamped with a heavy civil calender.

Unlike all of the other judges, Judge Shonefeld was unique in one facet of his political life. He never put off campaigning for re-election until voting time, but instead, made campaigning a daily practice the year round.

When each group of former aliens had been sworn

in and were still standing in front of his bench, Judge Shonfeld would drop his black judicial robe, step down into the body of the courtroom and personally shake the hand of each citizen.

He didn't welcome them as a judge, but warmly greeted each as an old friend. He overwhelmed them with his usual campaign speech:

"Congratulations. You are now American citizens, with all rights and privileges, especially the right to vote. When you step inside the voting booth you are going to be all alone and someday, when you glance down the list of candidates, you'll see the name...George W. Shonfeld. Make sure you pull down that handle."

CHAPTER 19

Bianchi Gets His License

Most newspapermen have a favorite story they enjoy telling about a political figure, known to all and always ready with lively quotes or a helping hand when needed.

Such a friend was Edmund "Pat" Brown, former governor who served from 1959 to 1967 and considered by most to be a "good guy." He took delight in telling how he acquired the name of "Pat" while an undergraduate at Lowell High School in San Francisco. He was cast as Patrick Henry, the lead role of the school's annual historical play and the name stuck. Pat made sure it did.

The near victim in this little drama about to unfold was Dal Bianchi, a kind and simple man who never before had heard of Pat Brown but was in dire need of a valid driver's license. For years Bianchi had a license; how he obtained it I never knew and didn't ask, for fear of embarrassing him.

He was a grave digger and gardener at the Italian Cemetery in Colma and never had an accident or traffic ticket. His big drawback was that he couldn't handle written English. Traffic signs and signals were never a problem...but a written test was impossible.

Meanwhile, the "Angel" who had been helping Bianchi for years past, suddenly dies, leaving poor Bianchi with a soon to expire license and panic stricken. He envisions himself as never being able to drive to his job and thus thrown out of work for the first time in his life.

He and his wife Suzie lived in North Beach, were close friends of my Mother-In-Law and since they came from the same town, Mondolfo, Italy, that made them pisanos, the same as being soul brothers.

Bianchi knew he had to get a new license as soon as possible and sent his wife to plead with my in-laws, to enlist any possible aid from me. In turn, my wife Irma is contacted, and naturally I end up with the assignment.

I drove to the Department of Motor Vehicles on Fell Street and explained to the director there is a section in the vehicle code that gives applicants the choice of a written or oral test. I was sure Bianchi's English was good enough to pass the oral exam. However, the director was most adamant and insisted he was short of help and didn't have to hold anything other than a written true or false test. The turn down was frigid and most final.

On the drive back to my office I kept thinking, "There must be something I can do...who is this guy's boss?" Then it dawned on me..."Pat Brown of course."

I called the governor's office and Pat came booming over the phone like he always did with his usual question, "Do you miss me?" "Oh God yes, you will never know," I answered and filled him in with Bianchi's license problem. The governor asked the name of the director at Fell Street and when I told him, he said, "Baron, call the guy in an hour and meanwhile I'll get the word to him."

Later I called the DMV and the director reacted as if I were the governor himself. "What's the most convenient time for you and Mr. Bianchi to come in?" he asked.

I set ten o'clock the following morning, and when we pulled up, the director himself was waiting inside the front door, his right hand extended and a silly grin on his face. He ushered us into his private office, sat Bianchi in his own desk chair and patiently showed him where to sign the new application. There was no examination and no questions were asked.

When Bianchi was signing his name, the director moved close and whispered in my ear, "Oh, Mr. Muller, when Sacramento calls, I hear so well."

When we drove away, Bianchi was ready to put Pat Brown on a pedestal.

CHAPTER 20

Case Of The Acid Bride

The most shocking crime in the Bay Area police files started in a fit of jealous anger, turned into a rage of slashing and burning fury, and after weeks of suffering, ended as an unbelievable murder. The main actors were the elegant Hajna Pillar and her new husband, Dr. Geza de Kaplany.

The tragedy started when Colonel Gyorgy Pillar, Captain of the Hungarian fencing team arrived in San Francisco in 1961 to prepare for the preliminary events of the upcoming Olympic games. He brought along his wife Illona and his beautiful daughter, Hajna, just turned twenty-four.

A couple of weeks later, the Colonel, always thought by his family to be in good health, suffered an unexpected heart attack and died instantly. Hajna and her mother were devastated and found themselves in a strange city with little money and few friends. Quick money was what they needed most and Hajna went looking for work.

At home in Hungary she had done some professional dancing and now her exceptional beauty made it a cinch to land a spot in the chorus at Bimbo's Nite Club of Columbus Avenue in North Beach. Any show manager would have been delighted to give her a gig. Just posing in the backdrop on stage and looking pretty would have been enough, but she showed such graceful foot work they put her in the front row center of the chorus line.

She was most poised and like the other chorines, poured herself into the skimpiest of costumes, driving most of the male patrons at the club bananas. She was a real hit.

Following the old world custom of observing the proper mourning period, Hajna and her mother knew they must begin living again and started attending a few Hungarian social events. It was at one of these affairs they first met Dr. de Kaplany. He showed much European charm with complete self assurance but was short, stuffy and showed no sense of humor.

When he was first introduced to Hajna it was love at first sight, for him especially, since she was from his country. He knew right away she would be the perfect wife for an ambitious young doctor.

He knew then he was going to marry her, but instead of courting her and showering her with favors, he followed the old and proper social customs and mores of his homeland and played up to her mother. Naturally, Mrs. Pillar was won over, delighted and especially proud that a doctor was interested in her Hajna. She knew that marrying a doctor was to reach the top of the social ladder.

Mama was overjoyed to give her blessing and the loving pair rushed into a whirlwind romance and were married a few months later. It was an elaborate wedding and friends on both sides agreed it was a perfect marriage.

Dr. de Kaplany was a practicing physician in Budapest, but since he had not been here long enough to complete his medical board tests he was not allowed to practice and had taken a post as an anesthesiologist at a hospital in San Jose.

They rented a neat apartment in the suburbs there, Hajna kept her job at the club and the newlyweds seemed headed for a happy life, so the mother testified later at the trial.

Then without any overt acts by his wife, the doctor became suspicious of the hours she spent in the city and made several surprise visits to the club. He was shocked to see her parading on stage in such skimpy costumes. To him it was shocking. He bitterly complained and she shrugged off his nagging with, "All the girls dress the same here...It's part of our act."

His visits to the club increased to more often, as did his moods of insane jealousy. He scolded that her bareness, so readily seen by other men, was a disgrace to his manhood. Proper wives in his world of upbringing, "Didn't do such things." Police believed this imagined shame apparently drove him out of his mind.

Later at his trial it was testified by several

witnesses that Hajna never gave him a single reason to be jealous of her deportment. It was further testified that when her act was over she never dallied at the club but came straight home alone.

The big blowup came on the afternoon of August 1, 1962, when his jealous moods turned to acts of horrible violence. Hajna was at home, preparing to leave for her job when the doctor burst in with his medical satchel stuffed with instruments of torture. He pulled on heavy rubber gloves to protect his precious hands and then took out vials of smoking acid, several new scalpels and a large rubber sheet that covered their bed.

Without saying a word he drew the drapes and shades, turned the radio to full volume to muffle any screams, and after stripping her nude, tossed her atop the bed and started his crazy butchery.

He slashed across her breasts with a scalpel, almost severing both nipples and then sliced a deep gouge the full length of her right chest. Hajna was fighting for her very life and screaming like a wounded animal, while the doctor, still without a word, kept up the attack and poured acid into the open wounds, her eyes and ears. He poured the remainder of the acid over her head and abdomen, taking special aim at her sexual organs.

Her screams eventually attracted the attention of other tenants in the building and when officers broke down the door, the doctor was still not finished with his horror. While he was being restrained and cuffed, he growled, "I'm a doctor...I know what I am doing and just how far I can go without killing her. She's not going to die...I know."

Hajna was still conscious while the police led the doctor away and took her to the nearest emergency hospital. Surgeons could not believe the torture that had been inflicted upon her and that she was still able to tell what had happened.

After emergency sedation in San Jose, doctors decided the best place for treatment would be St. Francis Hospital in San Francisco, noted as the outstanding burn center in the Bay Area. Her body was so badly seared and her pain so intense that nurses could not place her on ordinary sheets but had to use special sheer satin pads, carefully medicated to prevent any sticking to what was left of her skin. Her hair was so singed and discolored that most of it had to be cut away.

All this while, Mama was always at her bedside, petting her hand, crying pitifully and repeating over and over, "Look what that monster did to my beautiful Hajna."

Her wounds were so deep and intense that doctors could do little more than keep her heavily sedated and as comfortable as possible. Not once, from his prison cell in San Jose, did the doctor show any remorse nor ask about his wife who was slowly dying in agony. However, he did tell the jailors, "Now she's not going to be beautiful anymore...no man will ever give her a second look."

Photo by Barney Peterson

Dr. Geza de Kaplany and his bride Hanja at their wedding, February 6, 1963.

Her suffering went on for almost a month and then she mercifully passed away. It was early morning when the coroner's deputies picked up her body and returned it to the city morgue in the rear of the Hall of Justice. I was one of the first to learn of her death, only because I happened to be there and naturally called my office to report the incident. I told my City Editor Harry Press I was going over to take a look at the body.

He shouted back, "No Baron, for God's sake don't go. I heard when she was first transferred to St. Francis Hospital, the chief of staff of their burn center went to treat her and while making an examination was so overcome he had to leave her room and became ill in the hallway."

His warning made me more curious than ever and I had to see for myself. My contacts at the morgue wheeled the body into the viewing room and removed the covering sheet. The sight was a nightmare, much worse than I ever expected, but I didn't become ill, possibly because I was seeing her as a dead body and not a live and suffering human being. I never could understand how any man, especially a doctor, would perpetrate such acts of cruelty on his loving wife.

Her close cropped hair, making her look like a boy, had turned grotesque shades of orange, purple and dirty gray, while some of the deep body cuts had started to scab over and were a mess of horrible scars.

Most of her beautiful white skin, the body Mama was so proud of, had turned the color of darkened mahogany, similar to the finish of an antique grand piano. The eyes were blackened rings staring out of her expressionless face.

By the time Dr. de Kaplany was brought to trial in San Jose for murder, his devilment had attracted national news attention and was known as the Case of the Acid Bride.

Not once throughout the long trial did he show any signs of remorse and every day strutted into court with a smirk on his face, and took a seat at the counsel table, acting as if he were the attorney for the defense and not the defendant.

Mrs. Pillar attended every session of the trial and

was carefully searched before she was allowed to enter the courtroom. Everyone expected her to suddenly jump to her feet and shoot her son-in-law. That never happened.

When the defense opened its presentation of evidence, the doctor surprised everyone by swearing that his being was occupied by two different people...the good and loving husband who could never do such horrible things to his wife...and the devil, Pierre La Roche, solely responsible for the cruel murder. He kept on insisting the doctor was innocent. The jury instantly saw through this unique and most improbable ploy and was ready to vote a first degree murder verdict on the first ballot.

But then, the assistant district attorney went too far. He brought in colored pictures of Hajna's nude and disfigured body taken on an autopsy table in the coroner's office, had them greatly enlarged and passed around in the jury box. They all agreed that any man who could do such devilment had to be insane. They gave him life imprisonment.

He served in the State prison for eight years, had a record of good behavior and the Immigration Service, always anxious to be rid of him, returned him to his native country. However, the Hungarians didn't want him either and palmed him off to an undisclosed South American country, where it was reported he was planning to perform first aid services. The Examiner library has no record of whatever happened to Mrs. Pillar.

CHAPTER 21

Angelo Pavageau Murder Case: Another Senseless Killing

Never has it been my intention to present this book as a tale of horrors, but one more murder, so brutal and senseless must be retold because the case is still being featured by the press fifteen years after it happened. The killer, denied parole for the sixth time this summer is forever legally fighting to get out of prison.

The Angelo Pavageau murder execution was so horrible that even veteran homicide police were shocked, according to Inspector Frank Falzon who broke the case and arrested Pavageau. Inspector Falzon later handled the murder of Mayor George Moscone and Supervisor Harvey Milk by the former policeman and Supervisor, Dan White.

This story begins at midnight, a Friday evening in April, 1974. The victim Frank Carlson, 25, recently married and already promoted to the position of assistant manager of a chain food market in San Mateo, was preparing reports for his office at the dining room table of his modest home on Kansas Street on Potrero Hill. His attractive young wife, Annette, 25, was in the upstairs bedroom preparing to retire.

Pavageau, 40, a postal worker living in the area and unknown to the Carlsons, apparently used a piece of plastic to slip the front door lock, without making a sound and then suddenly placing himself in the dining room doorway, threatened young Carlson with a hunting knife.

Mrs. Carlson heard the commotion from her bedroom and rushed down to see her husband being savagely beaten about the head; in turn she was also threatened with the knife. He forced her to tie her husband to the chair in which he was sitting with napkins knotted around the arm rests, and then threw her to the floor and forced her to watch while he proceeded with his murderous attack.

Angelo Pavageau at the time of his arrest for murder.

He beat Carlson on the head so savagely with a hammer, a wooden chopping block and a tall ceramic vase filled with pennies, that each item broke. Pennies were scattered over the dining room rug. The chopping block, four inches thick and carved from a block of seasoned oak, split in half, as if it had been a piece of cigar box wood.

Seeing that the husband was dead, Pavageau

picked up Annette, all the while screaming for help, carried her up to the bedroom and repeatedly raped her, forcing her to commit acts of oral copulation and sodomy for an unbelievable period of three hours. She also suffered numerous broken bones, slit wrists and was strangled with a phone cord. In a corner of the room was a small wicker rocking chair with oak runners, something Annette had saved from her toys of childhood. First he beat her with a paper weight and then slammed her across the head with the rocker with so much force that one of the runner split in half, rendering her unconscious.

His final act, police believe, was an effort to hide his crime.

He poured gasoline over the bedroom and dining room walls where the murder was committed and set the home on fire. He left as quietly as he had entered. Fortunately, Mrs. Carlson revived quickly and squeezed through a smoldering window frame and dropped to the roof of a garage below, where she was rescued by firemen.

Inspector Falzon and I arrived on the scene at the same time, and following a quick overall look, we sped to San Francisco General Hospital where Annette was being prepared for surgery. Inspector Falzon needed answers and a full description of the killer before she went under the anesthetic. I followed to the outer room of surgery where he turned over his star, cuffs and police revolver for me to mind while he slipped into his surgical gown. When he came out later he shouted, "Now we have a full description of that guy and the horror and death he produced."

Pavageau's mistake was to pick up most of Mrs. Carlson's jewelry before he left and later trying to pawn it in the immediate area. Annette was a gifted artist and was able to provide police with detailed drawings of her jewelry that eventually led to his capture.

As every courtroom observer had predicted, Pavageau received the death sentence, later reduced to life in prison when the state death penalty laws were overturned by the Supreme Court.

Since his conviction, he has been denied parole

six times. The last turndown came this summer.

Mrs. Elizabeth Carlson, mother of the victim, looked on with dread and fear while the Board of Prison officials unanimously denied another parole hearing for at least two years.

"My family has lived with the knowledge there is always the possibility the prisoner may one day be released," Mrs. Carlson of Burlingame, told the board during its two hour hearing. "This fills me with dread."

Assistant District Attorney Theresa Welch of San Francisco said the viciousness of Pavageau's attack on the Carlson family was comparable to the murders committed by Charles Manson.

"It was more brutal than any execution we know of because of the time it took Frank Carlson to die," Welch added.

CHAPTER 22

Bridge Jumpers

Since the Golden Gate Bridge opened in 1939, 875 men and women have jumped to their deaths from the span, according to records of the California Highway Patrol. Members of the patrol insist this grim total is accurate, but the figure is greatly disputed by two veteran police reporters covering the Hall of Justice.

They are Malcolm Glover, a more than forty years plus staff member of The Examiner and Robert Popp, also a many year veteran of The Chronicle. They also cover the Coroner's Office and are responsible for covering all deaths on the bridges and in the Bay.

Both men contend the total today stands well over 1,200 deaths. They base this figure on the personal records Glover has been keeping during years past. Newspaper readers, the police and toll collectors long ago lost their interest in bridge jumpers. An accurate count naturally vanished with that lost interest. Today the jumper has to be most prominent, or a socialite, to rate even a few lines in the paper.

Following the ribbon cutting and grand opening, bridge officials were surprised to see how quickly the span became the popular mecca for persons bent on suicide.

Before the span opened, there was no particular location in San Francisco that was singled out and preferred by jumpers.

Some picked the phone company high rise, and others, for no apparent reason, took a dive from skyscrapers in the financial district. These locations turned into horrible tragedies when the jumpers landed atop a passing pedestrian, causing severe injury and sometimes death. Clean up was a big shocker. Whenever there was too much blood splatter and brain matter to pick up, the fire department was summoned to wash the gore down the nearest sewer. That problem never arose on either span.

Deputies in the Coroner's office think the bridge is chosen because of the available sidewalks on both sides and the assurance of sure death in the swift and deep running tides below. Another plus is the ample and inviting parking lots on both ends at the anchorage. The bay span has chalked up a number of suicides but nothing to compare to the astonishing list on the gate span. Some think the height of the railing encourages suicides.

Several cynical reporters covering the police beat became fascinated by the ever growing number of jump victims and thought it would be unusual to start a suicide pool. The list was fast nearing the half century mark and the promoters thought it would be bizarre to have a player pick the closest date to the time number 100 hit the water. The pool was open to anyone with a buck.

The contest took hold and right away became a hit, but the purpose of the pool was so repulsive to most that veteran reporters squelched the lottery.

CHAPTER 23

The Best Fire Department

The roar and thunder of speeding fire trucks and the thrill of covering multi-alarm fires has always fascinated me throughout my career as a newsman. I believe I would have become a fireman if I hadn't made it as a reporter.

I was born on Russian Hill, in San Francisco, a block down the hill from Engine No. 23 at Green and Leavenworth streets, one of the last companies to use horses. By 1922 the horses were gone, all replaced by motorized equipment that thundered along on solid rubber tires. All of the pumpers were nothing more than gas powered water pumps mounted on the body of a heavy truck. It wasn't until several years later that manufacturers of fire equipment hit upon the idea of using only one gasoline motor to, not only drive the engine, but power the pumps when the truck arrived at the scene of the fire. It was easily done by shifting a couple of levers and gears. I still recall the sights and sounds of the three horse drawn pumper, sparks shooting from its stack, plunging down the steep and cobbled Green Street hill. My grandfather operated the grocery store at the base of the hill and at the first sound of the bells and horses, he was at the intersection, blocking all traffic and the cable cars on Hyde Street. I used to think he was so brave.

When I was a lad in grammar school, I was fascinated by the attention from the crew at Co. #23 and loved to pet their horses, but I gained most of the background history of the department from veteran firemen I met when I began covering fires for the papers.

They told and retold the story of the great earthquake and fire of 1906, with the fire, that laster three days, doing the greater damage and burning down most of the town. The citizens vowed that would never happen again and established one of the most famous fire departments in the country, they were proud to tell.

The uniqueness of the department started with its great horses, an exclusive breed of Arabian for speed, Belgians for pulling strength, soon to be noted throughout the country as the San Francisco fire horse breed. They were also noted for their smarts and ability to count alarm bells, which is no exaggeration. Each fires station was assigned its own number of alarm bells and when the particular number of a house was struck, the horses instantly knew it, trotted out of their open ended stalls and stood rigid in the shafts of the engine, waiting to be hitched.

Next came another local fire department first. The harness and lines were suspended from a special rack in the ceiling, and when the horses were in place, the driver pulled a lever and the harness fell exactly into place on their backs.

It took only minutes to buckle the lines and go. The pumper engine had an ingenious and fast way of building up steam in a hurry. The fire box of the pumper had kindling wood, straw and coal, piled in the form of a pyramid and topped with a can of kerosene, with a lighted wick in the top. Before the huge front doors swung open, the pumper chief would tip over the can of burning kerosene, setting the pyramid ablaze. A full head of steam was usually ready by the time the company reached the fire. Returning the heavy engine and other equipment to the fire house, following the extinguishing of a blaze, was a tedious matter. At the base of the hill that housed the particular engine company, the team was stopped and two horses from the hose cart were hitched to the three pumper animals, making a five horse team. Usually the hill was so steep, they had to take the long way round to reach the top. When the heavy pumper was safely at home, the team was unhitched and sent down to pull up the hose cart.

Every fireman in the house had to learn to drive and handle the team. The reason...should the regular driver become injured, any man could bring the engine back to the house.

The teams, usually well matched pairs were kept in open box stalls on both sides of the station and were the pets of all in the neighborhood. Each horse had his own name tag tacked to the front of the stall.

People loved to bring them candy, apples and cubed sugar in that order. The firemen had to constantly watch to see the horses were not made ill through kindness and too much love-above all too much candy.

Whenever possible, fire houses, at the turn of the century were always built atop the city's major hills. That way, the horses never had to run up any major grade, but always down. Veteran firemen like to tell how citizens were amazed at the speed of the engines.

People knew the horses were swift but they didn't realize the team had to run so much faster down the cobbled hills to avoid being pushed in the rump and run over by the thundering engine behind them.

Following the great disaster of 1906, city engineers and fire officials realized the fire spread so

Baron Muller extinguishes the last of a freight shed fire with a water cannon, the Fire Department's most powerful piece of equipment.

far and so fast because of ruptures in the water mains and hydrant lines. Tank trucks would have been a great help, but they were not in use at that time.

To insure an adequate standby supply of water, huge cisterns, often called giant wells, were constructed underground at various intersections in the business and financial districts. Each cistern holds hundreds of gallons of water, is clearly marked in the intersection by a circle of cobble stones set in the pavement and is topped by a manhole cover that reads, "S.F.F.D." All are constructed as earthquake proof as possible. Should the need arise, firemen can easily remove the cast iron cover and drop a pump line to the adequate supply of water below.

Another supply of water for the Fire Department are the large tanks built into the hills on Twin Peaks Mountain. Their location close to the top of the peaks, give the system great pressure.

Today, like yesteryear, all fires are different. Each one has its own heroes, heartbreaks, deaths and tragedies. Almost every human emotion can be spotted at a fire, sometimes on the grim face of a fireman when he has rescued a pet cat or dog. His delight is overwhelming when he returns the pet to the arms of its owner. Every rescued animal had to have a name and if it wasn't available to us, we made one up.

Firemen too, I've often noticed, can be touched by emotions at a disastrous fire. I still recall the multi-alarm fire at the Ford Apartments on Mission Street. Eleven persons burned to death, were carried out by firemen and laid in a neat row on the sidewalk, awaiting the Coroner.

One young fireman I was watching appeared greatly upset by all the death around him. I knew he was a rookie because his heavy coat and helmet were sparkling new and it was obvious he was serving on his first body removal assignment. His face clearly showed how bothered he was. When he placed the last body in line on the sidewalk and covered it with a sheet, he walked to a dripping hydrant, bent over to avoid being seen and washed his new gloves under the steady drips. Still bent over, he walked to the

Fire Department steam pumper, circa 1900. This photo was taken in 1965 at a parade of early department vehicles.

nearest sewer and dropped the gloves through the grating.

Little dramas like this helped bring the stories alive, but we never became used to them. One group from the "old days" still remains active today after its inception more than eighty years ago. It's the Phoenix Society, an organization of dedicated fire buffs that respond, around the clock, to all multi-alarm fires. It is named for the mythical bird that, like San Francisco, rose from the ashes following the great quake and fire of 1906. A bronze sculpture of the bird sits atop the dome at City Hall.

Some members are so "hooked" they have alarm tickers in their bedrooms and turn out gear, helmets, boots and great coats in the trunks of their cars.

They do more than stand around like thrilled little boys and watch. They assist the firemen whenever possible, are aware of all the newest fire equipment and assist the press with their special knowledge. They often rate the various chiefs and are considered the best boosters of the department.

CHAPTER 24

Long Weekend At The Nudist Camp

More than once in a while we reporters had the pleasure of covering a real fun story. One of my best remembered features was the long weekend I spent at the nudist camp in the heart of the Santa Cruz Mountains. The back to nature event was held under the direction of the Sunny Terrace Nudist Colony. Four hundred delegates were invited to participate and they all showed up and some with a couple of friends in tow.

My editor had seen a short early announcement about the camp in the Santa Cruz paper, and because he was so hooked on unusual features he thought it would be different to do an "all out" piece on the camp. I got the assignment along with Eddie Murphy, our chief cameraman. The boss didn't ask if we wanted to go; he just told us. Murphy was a bit self conscious at first but I succeeded in talking him into going.

My first preparation was not to psyche myself up for the weekend adventure, that I didn't need, but to phone ahead to find out how we could get admitted.

The colony director said, "Sure, come on down...but remember you have to strip to get in." "Everything?" I asked, and he answered, "Yeah, but you can keep your shoes and socks as a place to pouch your cigarettes."

The camp was surrounded by a ten foot wooden fence to keep out curious intruders and peeping toms and was so well hidden amongst the redwoods we had trouble finding the entrance.

The director was waiting at the only gate and after he checked our press credentials he said, "Okay boys, this is where you strip." So, we squatted on the running board of our photo car and stripped, carefully folding our clothes on the back seat of the car.

"There is one restriction," he explained, "Take all

the pictures you want, but they must be developed in our dark room and we'll decide which photos you take out." We had to agree. Then he gave us a tour of the grounds, introduced us to everybody with the admonition that first names only were to be used. We were never to ask a delegate full name and address.

During the introductions I kept wondering what my physical reactions would be to this display of nudity. There were none. It felt the same as strolling the beach in my swim trunks.

All members in the camp, both children and adults, seemed to be at complete ease and never displayed signs of embarrassment or covering hand movements. I felt the same way and couldn't account for my lack of modesty.

Most of the nudists were young married couples and their small children, together with a number of gorgeous young women, who took no special interest in the press, never coming across with a second look. I was a healthy young man in my early twenties and didn't react accordingly.

In spite of the camp edict not to ask names, I was keenly interested to know where most of the people were from. That was easy. At night after everybody sacked out, I took my flashlight and peeked at the registration slips in the parked cars. Practically everyone was from the Los Angeles basin area.

Nights were pleasant and so balmy we could sleep with single blanket in hammocks, sometimes under pup tents or on piles of leaves raked from under the trees.

The big show of the day was to watch the girls run after a tennis ball or swat a volleyball. It was a new jiggling act for us and the girls paid no attention to our laughter.

At meal time we sat on benches, facing one another at long wooden tables. The waitresses were nude of course and were some of the girls we had watched earlier playing tennis. They leaned over our backs and served the food from the rear. It was a unique sensation to have something that felt like a warm piece of abalone rub across your spine and shoulder blades. The girls never said a thing, just kept on serving.

The only change in the undress code came when dancing was scheduled at night in the recreation room. It was boxer shorts for the men and swim trunks for the ladies. The children were always nude.

My cameraman, Eddie, took such clear and close-up photos that most of them never passed the censor in the camp darkroom. One photo that did pass and appeared later in our paper was an enlarged shot of myself seated on a hot boulder and hugging four girls, two in each arm. Naturally, it was shot from the rear.

When we returned to the paper we were surrounded by fellow staffers asking to know "everything" that went on at camp. We told them "everything", and quite naturally they wouldn't believe the things that never happened.

At home, my wife Irma had no objections to the weekend assignment, as I expected, but like the staffers, she wanted to hear how we passed the time in camp. However, she didn't like my story that ran the next day in the paper and led off with, "Spending the weekend at a nudist colony in the Santa Cruz Mountains caused me no more embarrassment than taking off my coat here in the office to write this story."

CHAPTER 25

Watching A Rare Heart Operation

It isn't often a reporter can recall a haunting story from long ago and wish the event had never taken place. It is a story I was most proud of at the time and was one of my major exclusives...witnessing the first open heart surgery on the Pacific Coast.

Just before the attack on Pearl Harbor, my editor received word that a Cleveland specialist, a pioneer in heart surgery, was scheduled to perform at San Francisco General Hospital, one of the most difficult operations then attempted. He had recently perfected a procedure for the relief of angina pectoris.

My assignment was to phone the doctor and get his permission to sit in and witness the surgery. I was young and inexperienced then and never dared to challenge a directive from the boss. How easily I could have put a man's life in jeopardy was a thought that never entered my mind.

The doctor was most cordial and talked freely about the coming surgery but turned me down cold, with the explanation he was bringing several colleagues and that would mean too many persons in the room. However he added he would not object to being interviewed following surgery and would take the time to explain the entire procedure in detail. That would not satisfy my editor. He insisted I get in the operating room.

From the phone conversation, I picked up the scheduled date and the name of the patient, a 23 year old youth from Vallejo, California, who had a condition best described as "pinched heart." I kept telling myself, "I must get in and watch that operation," without realizing the dire consequences that my unthoughtful presence could possibly create.

I know the layout of San Francisco General like my own home and it was easy to position myself in the hallway outside the surgeon's entrance to O.R. As I expected, the specialist came along with an entourage of invited observers and fellow doctors. They briskly walked into the ante-room and I joined step and brought up the rear.

In the clatter and chatter of the scrub room it was an easy matter to soap up and then feel inconspicuous and safe when I got behind a mask, cap and gown.

When we filed into surgery, I took a position well in the rear and when the "show started," I inched forward until I was close to the operating table.

The eminent specialist made a scalpel incision over the heart, widening the aperture a little at a time, cutting through blood vessels and stopping them off expertly. He explained everything as he proceeded. As the incision widened, two associates held back the side of the wound.

The room became stifling hot, especially from the bank of flood lights in the ceiling and the nurses kept mopping the doctor's forehead. I would have loved the same wipes.

The minutes passed slowly, everything was done with machine-like precision and the doctor asked from time to time, "How's his breathing?" Assured that everything was normal, he kept cutting, finally reaching the heart and delicately clearing away the surrounding membranes, exposing the organ to view. It was lying there in plain sight, thumping rapidly, beat following beat. The climax came next. A warm sterile sponge was placed on the surface of the heart and the doctor proceeded to make a cut into the organ itself. While the heart lay exposed, his sensitive hands guided instruments in removing blockage from the pericardial sac, permitting blood to resume its normal flow to the heart and throughout the body. Now the heat was unbearable and exhausting.

It was just past two hours before the last stitch was set in the incision and the team of watchers was unanimous in agreeing the patient's chance of living was a miracle of modern surgery. A few years earlier he would have faced inevitable death, they said.

I rushed out of surgery, dripping wet, still undetected, and sped to the office to write my big story. The home edition had it spread over page one with a headline that shouted, "REPORTER WITNESSES RARE HEART OPERATION."

That night when I re-read the story in the quiet of my living room, expecting to enjoy the scoop, I realized what a damn fool I was in crashing that operation. I could see that my brashness and desire for the big story could have easily set in motion a fatal disaster for the patient.

I asked myself, "What would have happened if I had fainted and fell across the surgeon's arms?" I felt ashamed and vowed..."never again." No exclusive story would ever be worth that risk.

CHAPTER 26

Our Own *Esprit de Corps*

Newspaper staff members usually have a good *esprit de corps.* Why? who knows? Perhaps it is to ensure their feeling of self preservation. It we thought a fellow staffer was unfairly treated, according to our standards, we took the means and "pulled the strings" to set the matter straight, or as we called it, "getting even."

This little vignette concerning a smoky fire in a first run movie house on Market Street, recalls the means we took to help a fellow staffer "get even." The buddy was Ernie Lenn, a next desk neighbor and a school mate from our undergraduate days at Stanford.

The theater was the Golden Gate at Market and Taylor streets, a combination of movies and vaudeville stage presentations. The time was the early fifties on a Saturday afternoon. The matinee had just started and the theater was packed with squealing kids.

Without any warning, a section of the balcony and loge seats suddenly filled with sickening clouds of dense smoke. The kids began screaming like banshees and the first battalion chiefs at the scene, recognized the potential danger and pulled a second alarm box, snarling all traffic at the busy intersection. It looked like the start of a big story.

Ernie rushed to the theater by cab and began phoning in a vivid story. Like the fireman, he too sensed the same potential for panic amongst the children, not from the flames but the choking smoke.

All the while he was dictating his story to a stenographer on the phone, he was unaware the theater's press agent was standing near by, listening to every lurid detail. The firemen quickly extinguished the fire, cleared out smoke and felt they had averted a situation that could have been most disastrous.

When our next edition hit the downtown street corners the fire was spread across the top line. Within minutes the press agent came roaring into the office, bitching that Ernie had blown a "nothing story" out of all proportions and demanded a retraction. He argued that, in the future, movie goers might think of the theater as a "fire trap" and stay away. His chief argument was that the theater was one of our major advertisers.

He didn't get the retraction. Instead, Ernie, much to his embarrassment, got a bawling out in the middle of the city room. That chew-out had to be reversed, we felt, and it was, sooner than any of us expected.

I was assigned to that old Hall of Justice on Kearny Street, covering the traffic court of Judge Daniel S. O'Brien.

Every morning, before court opened, I would check the calendar for prominent names, or anybody worthy of a story. On this particular morning, I was delighted to see the name of our "friendly" press agent, charged with speeding. I figured it would even the score to have the judge send him to traffic school for six nights, a sentence most defendants hated.

The judge and I got along well because he liked my court stories that were most often written in his favor. One of his favorite admonitions to an offender, before pronouncing sentence was, "If you had behaved yourself you wouldn't be here. Bring your old clothes and a tooth brush tomorrow, you're going to jail."

The judge laughed and slapped his knee when I asked him in the quiet of his chambers to send the theater agent to traffic school. After Judge O'Brien heard the full story he said, "I'll double it." And he did.

At the first court recess I phoned Ernie and told him of the "sentence." He never forgot and often retold the incident. The press agent probably did too and never knew why the judge gave him such a stiff jolt.

CHAPTER 27

Joe DiMaggio Marries Marilyn

One of my important and least expected scoops happened at noon, January 15, 1954, when Joe Di-Maggio and Marilyn Monroe were married at City Hall.

I was upstairs in the fourth floor Superior Court covering a dull probate matter when the judge unexpectedly called an early noon recess and everybody left for lunch. At that time the elevators had not yet been converted to push button controls and were still manually operated. Later after the switch over and the men were replaced by electronic push buttons, we lost many good stories. The male operators saw who came and went and had the news sense to spot a good story.

As I was leaving the lift on the main floor, Teddy Weiss, a veteran operator and the chief dispatcher grabbed my arm and whispered, "Baron, I just took Joe DiMaggio and Marilyn Monroe up to Judge Peery's court." I thanked him with a heavy backslap and back upstairs I rushed to the third floor court of Municipal Judge Charles S. Peery. The courtroom was empty. I could hear voices and much laughter coming from his chambers.

I knew Judge Peery well enough to walk in, and there, sitting on the judge's couch and holding hands were Joe and Marilyn. She was almost smothered in orchids.

Joe, the retired Yankee slugger and Marilyn, who made most young men ache just by walking by, had been dating for months and the gossip columnists were suspecting a marriage in the future. No date had been set and here it was about to happen.

This would be the second time for Joe. In the early 30's he married Dorothy Arnold, a charming newcomer to films with potential stardom. The ceremony had an elaborate Hollywood setting at Sts. Peter and Paul Catholic Church, the Italian cathedral in North Beach. The marriage didn't last

Joe DiMaggio and Marilyn Monroe on their wedding day, January 15, 1954.

too long, however, Dorothy did present Joe with a
son, Joe, Jr. Years later he made the papers when he
joined the Marines and then dropped out of the news.
No one claims to know where he is today.

Meanwhile in chambers, the bridal party was
taking places before the judge. Of course, Marilyn
had a looker as maid of honor and best man was
Joe's long time buddy, Reno Barsocchini, well known
bar and grill operator in the financial district.
Looking on was "Lefty" O'Doul and his wife.

"Lefty," a national figure in baseball, and batting
record holder, was Joe's first coach here with the
Seals, a local minor league team. Lefty was one of
the first baseball coaches to see the great potential in
DiMaggio and early on sold him to the Yankees.

When the judge started the short and informal
ceremony, I stood at the judge's desk, phoning in a
play by play to my office. There were several short
laughs when Marilyn squeaked her, "I do." then it
was all hugs, kisses and congratulations.

While the reception was going on, my story
reached the wire services and within minutes the
court was overrun with reporters and cameramen,
making the most of an unexpected event. They
followed the bridal party to Fisherman's Wharf and
interrupted the nuptial lunch.

Our home edition headlines that afternoon gave
me a big lift, but you can't drool too long over an
exclusive story. Another will be expected next
week...or even sooner.

No squawk was forthcoming from the city desk
next day when I turned in my expense account,
listing half a case of Cutty Sark scotch for Teddy.

As a youth, and later, a long time in his player
days, Joe usually had nothing to say and was often
regarded as a loner. Once he did say, "His bat spoke
for him." During his years with the Yankees, Joe's
best pals were Tony "Push 'em up Tony" Lazzeri and
Frank "The Crow" Cosetti. On road games, Joe and
Tony were roommates.

An after dinner story that had made the rounds
at "Old Timers Nights," and is still being retold
today, tells of the time Joe, Tony and Frank drove
cross country in Tony's car to start spring training at

a camp in Florida. Joe is said to have sprawled across the back seat, the whole trip, saying nothing. When they neared Miami, Joe grunted he wanted out to visit a friend.

Joe closed the car door without a word of "thank you" or "good-bye." Lazzeri turned to Crosetti and said, "Talkative...Isn't he?"

CHAPTER 28

President Johnson Gets Sworn In

In the long ago days while I was a senior student at Galileo High School, San Francisco, one of the prerequisites for a certificate of graduation was a course in Civics. Today it's called Government or Social Studies. The class was limited to fourth year students and taught by Georgia Hawkins, Vice Principal and Dean of Girls.

She was tough and it was her special way of holding our attention and respect for her, or so we thought. On the second day of class she sat us down, gave a loud grunt and greeted us with this warning, "No one here looks like presidential material to me, but all my classes in the past have learned the Presidential Oath of Office and you're going to learn it too. There will be no exceptions. That includes written and oral exams before I'll let you out of here."

I knew it was useless material I would never use and since it was a requirement to get out of her class, I hunkered down and learned the thing.

Thirty-five years later, on November 22, 1963, a special day in Dallas, I gave a silent thanks to my memories of Dean Hawkins for making me so knowledgeable.

President Kennedy had just been assassinated and Lyndon Johnson was nervously waiting in the main cabin of Air Force One to be sworn in as the thirty-sixth president.

Federal District Judge Sara Hughes was rushed from her court in Dallas to administer the oath.

Our news staff crowded a TV set in the news room watching the drama and a big slice of history too, as it unfolded on the screen.

Lady Bird Johnson took her place beside her husband and remained mute. Jackie Kennedy, still in her blood stained suit, lined up on the other side and had full control of her emotions. Confusion was everywhere. A squad of Secret Service agents tightly circled the little group, anxious to get the proceedings finished and return the new president to the safety of Washington. The swearing in never started and the delay was agonizing to all.

My editor came running from his office shouting, "What in hell is holding up the big show? Our home edition can't wait a minute longer."

We explained that the judge forgot to bring along the oath and had sent an aide back to the courthouse to get a copy.

"Oh shellac," he snapped. "Our edition can't wait. Does anyone know the damned oath?" When I volunteered, "I did," he said, "Write it for a special box for page one."

I typed, "I solemnly swear that I will faithfully execute the office of President of the United Stated and will, to the best of my ability, preserve, protect and defend the Constitution of the United States. So help me God."

When the home edition came off the press and the office quieted, the editor walked over and asked, "Baron, how in the hell did you know that?" I told him about Georgia Hawkins and her class at Galileo. "They don't make that kind of teacher anymore."

CHAPTER 29

Getting Out of The Trenches

It was never a bore going to the paper everyday and never did I wish, or even think I should have gone into some other line of work. My job was fascinating. Many times I told my wife Irma, "Honey, think how lucky I am. I enjoy what I'm doing and getting paid for it too!"

Being happy at work made the years skip by uncounted. The idea of "hanging it up" never entered my thoughts and I believed and hoped, the job would go on forever. But that was not to be.

In late 1978, a small and inflamed growth appeared on my lower left gum and jaw and I found myself in Presbyterian Hospital, San Francisco, being prepped for major surgery. I was scared to death and imagined the worst.

Later in the recovery room my surgeon, Dr. James C. Klein, shook me awake to tell me the best possible news, "Baron, I cut it out and threw it in the bucket...you're fine." And I was.

Later when my wife accompanied me to the doctor's office for a final check-over, Dr. Klein surprised us with the suggestion that I retire. "Baron, don't you think you've spent enough time in the trenches? Get out while you're ahead." My wife really seconded his advice and they both made sure I agreed. I couldn't do otherwise.

The touching part came later when I returned to the Examiner, handed in my written resignation and said my good-byes to the staffers. To me, they were all members of my family. That wasn't to be the end.

On Saturday evening, March 24, 1979, the Examiner and staff honored me with a gala retirement dinner in the Palm Court of the Sheraton Palace Hotel. Mayor Dianne Feinstein was honorary chairperson along with Malcolm Glover of the Examiner and Robert Popp of the Chronicle as co-chairmen. Al Graf, the bail bondsman, and well known by everyone, introduced the speakers and served as Master of Ceremonies.

Baron Muller was honored with the "Foster City Volunteer of the Year" award by the Foster City Chamber of Commerce in 1982.

The dinner had been leaked to me as a "small party" and when I walked in and saw the huge turnout I couldn't believe the wondrous surprise. Seated for dinner were scores of Municipal and Superior judges, three former police chiefs, two fire chiefs and staff, the Districy Attorney and the Public Defenders and several tables of attorneys. In all, filling up the room were two hundred writing and non-writing friends and family.

It was hard to keep back tears as I told them how pleased I was to see them all and I couldn't imagine anyone paying $22.50 to bid me farewell and wish me good health in retirement.

The final speech was made by William Conroy, head of the Disaster Corps, former police captain and noted after dinner speaker. He closed the affair with a bang when he explained, "Baron is the only person I know who could come here tonight with his children...his wife...and his MADAM."

N°. 056

EXTRA   EXTRA   EXTRA   EXTRA

BARON MULLER RETIREMENT DINNER

GARDEN COURT, SHERATON PALACE

635 MARKET STREET, SAN FRANCISCO

SATURDAY, MARCH 24, 1979

No-Host Cocktails 6:30 p.m. • Dinner 7:30 p.m.

MAYOR DIANE FEINSTEIN, Honorary Chairperson
AL GRAF, Chairman
MALCOLM GLOVER & ROBERT POPP, Co-Chairmen
$22.50 per person

Baron Muller "...gets out of the trenches."

Sally Stanford in 1979 when she spoke at Muller's retirement party.

About The Author

A native San Franciscan, Baron Muller was born and raised on Russian Hill, the exact corner where his father was reared, married and started his family.

After attending local schools and graduating from Stanford University, Muller started his writing career on the staff of the San Francisco News, a Scripps-Howard paper. From there he merged with the News-Call Bulletin and later the Examiner, without ever leaving home and covering a span of 42 years.   He still enjoys talking about his favorite stories and what a pleasure it was to report to work every morning.

Years later when his wonderful Italian mother-in-law came to live with him and his wife Irma, he loved to boast that "he had the two best Italian cooks in the city." When the mother-in-law died in their Sunset District home, the place held so many memories that Mrs. Muller thought it best they move. The year was 1965 and the Mullers became pioneers of Foster City.

After Baron retired from the Examiner in 1980, he was surprised to be invited by Peggy Ankerbrand, Executive Vice President, to become an Ambassador of the Foster City Chamber of Commerce. He readily accepted and took such a keen interest in this new field that he was elected a Director of the Chamber.

At the start of this new and second career, he was asked to give the "Speech of Welcome" at all Ribbon Cuttings for new businesses, entrepreneurs and professional people celebrating their entrance into the Chamber and Foster City.

Never giving the same speech twice, that number of greetings has now grown into nearly 100 hearty welcomes. He often reminds his friends at the Chamber that he has only one thing to sell: "Foster City." ...And now, his book, too.

INDEX

Aaron, April, 44, 45
Air Force One, 94
Alcatraz Island, 35
Ankerbrand, Peggy, 100
Arnold, Dorothy, 90, 92
Baron (horse), 57
Barsocchini, 92
Bay Bridge, 22, 24
Bianchi, Dal, 62, 63
Bianchi, Suzi, 62
Bimbo's Nite Club, 64
Brier, Royce, 34
Brisbane, Arthur, 33
Brown, Edmund "Pat," 62, 63
Brown, Mike (Deputy Coroner), 40
Budapest, 65
Burkhardt, W. N. "Bill," 3, 14
Burlingame, 73
Busby, Mable Janis, 9
Butler, John (Captain, Department Secretary), 46
Cahill, Thomas J. (Chief of Police), 46
California Highway Patrol, 74
Capt. Ahab, 34-36
Carlson, Annette, 70, 72
Carlson, Elizabeth, 73
Carlson, Frank, 70, 71, 73
Case of the Acid Bride, 64-69
Cauthorn, Joseph, 59, 60
Central Emergency Hospital, 19, 20
Chase, Richard, 32, 34, 36
Chessman, Carl, 55
Chinatown, 17
Christopher, George (Mayor), 46
Chronicle, 2, 33, 74
"City Editor," 1
City Hall, 17, 59, 60, 90
Civic Center, 19, 28
Cliff House, 57
Colma, 62
Conroy, William, 98
Cosetti, Frank "The Crow", 92
Crocker Bank, 1
Davis, Richard Harding, 1
de Kaplany, Dr. Geza, 64-69
DeMaggio, Joe, 90, 92
Disneyland, 46
Doran, Vern, 40, 42
Downey, Sheridan, 60
Dreamland Auditorium, 39
Dullea, Charles W. (Captain of Inspectors), 39, 40, 42
Dullea, Monsignor Charles, 42
Dunne, Frank (Superior Judge), 42
East Bay, 22

Egan, Frank, 38-41
Embarcadero, 18
"Empress of Britain," 13
Examiner, 2, 74, 96, 100
Fairmont Hotel, 27, 36
Falzon, Frank (Inspector), 70, 72
Farralones, 18
Federal Courts, 17
Federal Immigration Service, 59
Feinstein, Dianne (Mayor), 96
Fisherman's Wharf, 92
Flood Building, 38
Ford Apartments, 79
Foster City, 100
Foster City Chamber of Commerce, 100
Frank Egan Murder Case, 38
Franklin Savings and Loan Society, 1
"Front Page," 1
Gable, Clark, 3
Galileo High School, 1, 94, 95
Geary Street, 6
Geiger, Dr. Jacob "Jake", 19
Glover, Malcolm, 74, 96
Gold Rush, 17
Golden Gate Bridge, 22, 23, 74
Golden Gate Park, 44, 57
Golden Gate Theater, 88
Grace Cathedral, 36
Graf, Al, 96
Graham, Barbara, 55
Gump, Robert Livingston, 9
Gump, Sally Stanford, 9
Hall of Justice, 17, 26, 38, 42, 46, 68, 74, 89
Hallinen, Terrance, 43
Hallinen, Vincent, 42, 43
Hart, Brook, 29, 30
Hart's Department store, 29
Hawkins, Georgia, 94, 95
Hearst, William Randolph, 13, 14
Holmes, John, 29
Hoover, President Herbert, 26, 27
Houseman, Dr. Nathan, 38, 39, 43
Hughes, Mrs. Jesse Scott, 38-41
Hughes, Sara (Federal District Judge), 94
Islam Temple Shrine, 6
Italian Cemetary, 62
Johnson, Lady Bird, 94
Johnson, President Lyndon, 94
Kennedy, Jackie, 94
Kennedy, President John F., 94
Key system electric trains, 24
Khrushchev, Nikita, 46
Klein, Dr. James C., 96
Knowland, William, 60
La Roche, Pierre, 69
Lake County, 57
Lantis, Zoe Dell, 34-36

Lazzeri, Tony "Push 'em up Tony", 92
Lee, Martin (Chief of Inspectors), 57
Lenn, Ernie, 88, 89
Lowell High School, 62
Maddox, Parker, 40
Manson, Charles, 73
Marin County, 9, 22, 53
Marina District, 3
Milk, (Supervisor) Harvey, 70
Milpitas, 29
Monroe, Marilyn, 90, 92
Morgan, Edmond P. (Superior Court Judge), 59, 60
Moscone, (Mayor) George, 70
Muller, Irma, 62, 84, 96, 100
Murphy, Eddie (cameraman), 53, 82, 84
News-Call Bulletin, 2, 100
Newspaper Guild, 3
Nob Hill, 27, 28, 36
North (Marin) tower, 24
North Beach, 90
O'Brien, Daniel S. (Judge), 89
O'Doul, "Lefty", 92
Pacific Coast, 18
Pacific Union Club, 28
Palo Alto, 1, 19, 26
Pavageau, Angelo, 70-72
Pearl Harbor, 85
Peery, Charles S. (Judge), 90
Phelan Building, 38
Phoenix Society, 80
Pillar, Colonel Gyorgy, 64
Pillar, Hajna, 64-69
Pillar, Illona, 64, 65, 67-69
Popp, Robert, 74, 96
Potrero Hill, 70
Presbyterian Hospital, 96
Presidential Oath of Office, 94, 95
Presidio Hills, 24
Press Club, 11, 53
Press, Harry, 46, 68
Public Utilities, 17
Question Man column, 21
Rapp, Marsha, 9
Reagan, President Ronald, 26, 28
Reno, 9
Robinson's Pet Shop, 36
Rolph, Governor James "Sunny Jim", 33
Roosevelt, President Franklin, 26, 33
Russian Hill, 76, 100
Sacramento, 28
Saint Clair Hotel, 33
San Francisco Bay, 17
San Francisco fire horse breed, 77
San Francisco General Hospital, 19, 72, 85
San Francisco News, 2, 3, 13, 33, 54, 59, 100
San Jose, 29, 30, 33, 34, 38, 44, 65-68
San Juan Hill, 26
San Mateo, 70
San Mateo Bridge, 30
San Quentin Prison, 48, 50, 55
San Rafael, 53

San Simeon, 13, 14
Santa Cruz, 82
Santa Cruz Mountains, 82, 84
Sausalito, 11
Schmaltz, 34, 35
Scripps Howard paper, 2, 100
Shaw, George, 13, 14
Sheraton Palace Hotel, 96
Shonefeld, George Washington (Superior Court Judge), 60, 61
Smith, Court (San Quentin Warden), 51, 53
Sontheimer, Morton, 3, 5, 11, 13-15, 21, 30, 32
South (San Francisco) tower, 24
Southern Pacific railroad, 24
St. Francis Hospital, 66, 68
St. Francis Hotel, 5, 36
St. James Park, 30, 32
Stanford Chapel, 19
Stanford Review, 12
Stanford, Sally, 6, 8, 9-12
Stanford University, 1, 2, 8, 12, 26, 88, 100
State Board of Medical Examiners, 43
State Public Utilities Commission, 12
Sts. Peter and Paul Catholic Church, 90
Sunny Terrace Nudist Colony, 82
Tenderloin, 28
The City of Paris, 59
"The Daily," 2
The Valhalla, 9, 11
Thurmond, Thomas, 29
Tinnen, Albert, 40, 42
Treasure Island, 34, 36
Truman, President Harry, 27
Twin Peaks Mountain, 79
Union Square Garage, 36
University of San Francisco, 42
Vallejo, 85
Verdier, Paul, 59, 60
Vietnam, 18
Vigilantes, 29
Walker, Stanley, 1
Weiss, Teddy, 90
Welch, Theresa (Assistant District Attorney), 73
Wells Fargo, 1
West, George, 21
West, Mae, 8
White, Dan, 70
World War II, 59
Wright, Guy, 59
Writers Union, 3